What I've Learned

Esquire

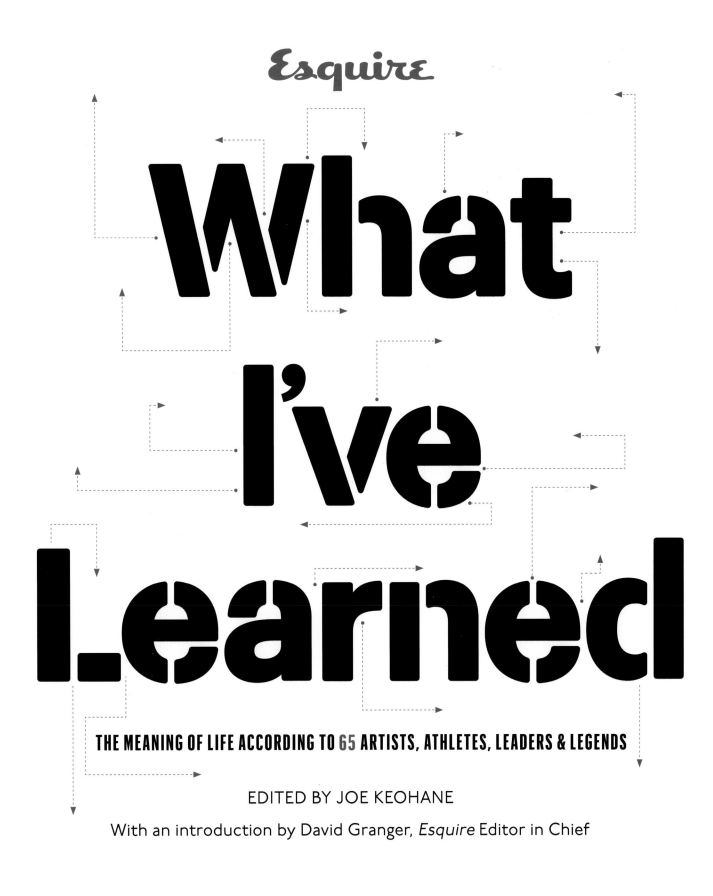

What I've Learned

THE MEANING OF LIFE ACCORDING TO 65 ARTISTS, ATHLETES, LEADERS & LEGENDS

EDITED BY JOE KEOHANE

With an introduction by David Granger, *Esquire* Editor in Chief

HEARST BOOKS
New York

CONTENTS

INTRODUCTION

FOR THE LAST 18 YEARS, very nearly every issue of Esquire has run a feature we call *What I've Learned*. It was born in a conference room, named by deputy editor Peter Griffin, and executed the first time by one of our writers, Mike Sager. The first subject was the actor Rod Steiger, who showed up for the interview with aphorisms already written out on several pages of a tattered legal pad. "Fantasies of success should never precede endeavor" was the first nugget he offered, and the first one we published.

On its surface, What I've Learned is the simplest of magazine stories. We (actually, most often it's writer at large Cal Fussman) seek out a person who has lived an extraordinary life, and, in conversations that can range from 60 minutes to a couple dozen hours (that was Al Pacino in 2002), we try to extract from them the wisdom that has accrued over a life interestingly lived. But it goes deeper than a simple conversation. We do a lot of research, avoid topics that might lead the subject into well-trod conversations he or she has already had, throw a couple curveballs, and, most of all: *listen.*

It's amazing what happens in the moments in which the interviewer simply says nothing at all and lets the subject talk. Looking back at the pieces in this book, which ran in the magazine from 2009 to early 2015, I kept finding sentences that have become irreversibly embedded in my brain. Like when Keith Olbermann said to Cal, "I've never fought the word 'genius' when people have said that about me." I use that in jest to this day. And when Chevy Chase advised us to "Make as much noise as possible and break as few bones as you can," and Amy Schumer argued that "the moments that make life worth living are when things are at their worst and you find a way to laugh," and Kevin Hart helped solve the riddle of how exactly one gets thrown out of a celebrity basketball game: "You get naked. Start taking your clothes off and throw your shoe at the ref."

The subjects of these interviews come from every discipline. Politicians, actors, geniuses, legendary athletes, just plain legends, pop stars, sex therapists (well, just one of those), writers, composers, a former President of the United States, directors, and a handful of our own readers. From what they've learned, we learn. And because we experience their words freed from conversational context, they take on the weight and bulk of certainty. Or something even greater. As a reader wrote recently: "I've come to believe that What I've Learned feeds, guides, comforts, advises, and directs the human spirit, just as profoundly as any text considered sacred by humanity."

Amen. It's intensely comforting to learn, as you will in the pages that follow, that most of the problems and stresses and disappointments of your life are also common to many of the most extraordinary people alive. We all have doubt, we all stumble and, in the example of the 65 people in this book and the hundreds who have participated over the last 18 years, what we learn is that the vast majority of life's obstacles are surmountable and, in fact, that it is our challenges that most often lead us to moments of triumph.

David Granger, Editor in Chief, *Esquire*
APRIL 1, 2015

50 CENT

MUSICIAN, NEW YORK CITY • *Interviewed by Ross McCammon*

>**IT'S FIFTY,** not Fiddy.

>**MY MOM CHOSE** the lifestyle because she didn't choose welfare. Every time I seen her, it felt like Christmas. Everything that was nice in my life was gone when she left, and the only people I saw that had nice things were people from the lifestyle. And they'd look at me and go, *Why you look like that? Why your shoes run-down?*

>**WHAT LED MY MOM** into the lifestyle that got her killed was what led me into the lifestyle: to prevent needing things so much.

>**IF I'D HAD A CHOICE,** I would've been a college kid. I would've majored in business.

>**SOMETIMES** you *do* need to convince yourself through convincing others.

>**I NEVER SAW DRUG USE** as a good option. I'd rather have an additional ten dollars than smoke. It wasn't a decision to not smoke weed. It was a decision to hustle. It was a business decision.

>**HUSTLING WAS** my internship.

>**BEING SHOT DEFINES** how strong I am. It prepares you for the confusion of being an artist.

>**THE ADRENALINE** doesn't allow the bullets to hurt as much as being afraid hurts.

>**COLUMBIA RECORDS** shied away from me. They were afraid of someone who would actually come from the real shit. You know what happens right after you assess me being shot? You go, *Wow, so he's really down there with the people who will just shoot you nine times? Will they shoot me, too?* Why sell 50 when we can sell Kanye?

>**THERE'S PEOPLE** who are considered intelligent who are idiots.

>**PEOPLE WHO** raise their hands deserve to be ahead of people who don't.

>**MONEY IS FREEDOM.** Money is a private plane. Money is no metal detection.

>**I SIGN AUTOGRAPHS** because there will be a moment when no one asks me to.

>**DON'T WAIT** for them to tell you. Tell them.

>**THERE ARE TOO MANY** entrepreneurs. We need the worker to make the process function properly.

>**THE FIRST TIME** I felt rich was when I had $80,000 inside my house. I saw it as a means to more money.

>**MONEY IS NOT** going to make you happy. A new idea is what makes you happy.

>**WHEN I GOT SHOT,** it was a $5,000 exchange. The price of a life is cheap.

>**OBAMA TAKES** away the excuses.

>**THE BEST BUSINESSMEN** in the world make a bad deal sometimes. And it's not usually in a boardroom. Most of them marry the wrong woman. That business deal is the worst business deal of all.

>**ALL THE WOMEN** have contributed to my success. Every one.

>**IN MY HOUSE,** Carmelo Anthony is bigger than 50 Cent.

>**MY SON IS** more important to me than I am to him.

>**ALWAYS HAVE** bail money.

>**CURTIS JACKSON.** I identify with the name. When I look in the mirror, I see Curtis.

>**AM I AN HONEST MAN?** I'm a selectively honest man.

>**AM I BEING HONEST RIGHT** now? Yeah. Most people would answer that question with a yes. Even the liars.

>**JAY-Z IS** as politically correct as some of the politicians. He's safe. There's points when you're acquiring financing, you make adjustments. He's made those adjustments. It's his choice. For me, it's not a necessity.

>**WHEN YOU'RE SAFE,** people start walking on the stage because they feel safe with you. People don't walk on the stage at my shows.

>**AIR JORDAN.** Tiger Woods. You know how a person is made for something? Eminem is made for hip-hop. The best rapper is a white man.

>**MY MUSIC IS A SOUNDTRACK.** The film is my life. My music matches things I've experienced or felt. Even if the whole thing is made up.

>**WHEN YOU GET HURT** as bad as I got hurt, the idea of hurting someone as bad as they hurt you is no longer out of the question.

>**DEPRESSION** is a luxury I still can't afford.

>**I LIKE GENERALS.** I like Napoleon. I like strategy. The majority of them are praised for mass destruction, but it's exciting to see how it comes to the mind mentally.

>**RAP ARTISTS ARE LIKE FIGHTERS.** They don't need a coach to call them champ for them to believe it.

>**YOU NEED** a respectable opponent, but you don't have to respect 'em. In the end you're gonna finish 'em anyway, right?

BIO
BORN CURTIS JAMES JACKSON III, JULY 6, 1975, NEW YORK CITY • Appeared in the January 2010 issue

>Recorded six albums, including *Get Rich or Die Tryin'*, *Curtis*, and *Animal Ambition*
>Won a Grammy in 2009 for "Crack a Bottle" with Eminem and Dr. Dre
>Founded the energy drink company Street King Energy

TIM ALLEN

ACTOR, LOS ANGELES ◆ *Interviewed by Cal Fussman*

>USE A SCREWDRIVER INSTEAD OF A HAMMER. Try to untighten the nut with your hand. Utilize the path of least resistance first.

>I BLEND MEMORIES. I blend them into one that's funny. I exaggerate to clarify.

>BEING WEALTHY when no one else is is like being the only one at the party with a drink.

>YOU DON'T KNOW WHAT PEOPLE are really like until they're under a lot of stress.

>IN POLITICS, there's compromise and everyone feels like shit. In marriage, compromise nurtures the relationship.

>MY COMEDY IS NOT MINE. It's a gift. I'm not that smart.

>MY GRANDMA ONCE TOLD ME, "Don't confuse your perceptivity with intelligence."

>WHEN SOMEBODY tells you they're not very smart, they're saying exactly the opposite.

>I HAVE IRRATIONAL FEARS, and they all go back to losing my father as a kid. I've never gotten over it. One day my father was there, the next he wasn't, and there was no going back. There's no "I'll be better, God. Now I know I shouldn't eat candy." As children, your world is yours. That day taught me that it's really not your world. Somebody else is in control—fate, God, whatever it is. It is not your show. And the show can be brutal. Brutal in its coldness. Brutal in its love and affection. Shit can hit you straight between the eyes and you never saw it coming, even when you were looking straight ahead.

>A CAR CROSSED TWO LANES OF TRAFFIC, flipped, and landed on my dad's car. I don't blame cars. My dad loved cars. I don't have many memories of my dad. The love of cars is all I have of him, really.

>ONE OF THE BEST PIECES OF ADVICE my mother gave me was "Make your bed in other people's homes. That way you get invited back."

>MY STEPFATHER STEPPED IN where no man would've stepped in—six kids, five of them boys—and that's heroic.

>I KNOW IT SOUNDS ODD, but I want to make a Rolex-quality screwdriver.

>THE UNFAIRNESS OF LIFE is indicative of trees. I planted twenty trees on the same block. It's so fucking weird. Six became huge. One is giant. And there are some little shitty ones. Same soil. Same water. Same seed. But those little ones just don't grow. I can't explain it.

>I'M SAD FOR ADULTS WHO want to be children. And children who want to be adults.

>ONE OF MY GOALS IS to plant five thousand trees in L. A. You think it's easy? I've never seen more red tape than when it comes to planting trees.

>THE EGO IS LIKE A KID in the basement: It's best to keep him busy.

>SOMETIMES YOU GET THE SENSE that the Creator is getting to that point of, "Yeah, we might have to reboot."

>BE WARY OF LISTENING to stories secondhand.

>AS THE CHINESE WILL TELL YOU, history depends on your point of view.

>I'M A VERY BAD STUDENT, but a great learner.

>WHEN I WENT TO JAIL, reality hit so hard that it took my breath away, took my stance away, took my strength away. I was there buck naked, humiliated, sitting in my own crap and urine—this is a metaphor. My ego had run off. Your ego is the biggest coward.

>THE LAW WAS PASSED to teach people a lesson. Selling more than 650 grams of cocaine got you life in prison. They thought it would be a deterrent. It wasn't. I was put in a holding cell with twenty other guys—we had to crap in the same crapper in the middle of the room—and I just told myself, I can't do this for seven and a half years. I want to kill myself.

>THAT'S WHEN THE COMIC IN ME APPEARED. The comic said, "Have you ever killed yourself before? Do you know how it works? Let me tell you how it's going to end up: You're gonna get it wrong and end up hanging a few inches off the ground with your shirt just over your ears, going: 'Oh, fuck. Somebody help me . . .' You're gonna hang like an idiot for an hour with everybody just looking at you." The image of my head straining with the shirt over my ears made me laugh. The comic in me showed up, the purest form, and saved my life.

>I DO MY BEST to stay away from expectations.

>VERY RARELY DO WE LISTEN to the wisdom of people who go before us. I haven't found a wise man. Do you know a wise man, right now?

>IF YOU WERE TOLD THE END at the beginning, you wouldn't have to travel.

BIO BORN JUNE 13, 1953, DENVER ◆ *Interviewed August 27, 2011*

>One of nine siblings
>Made a name for himself by cracking jokes about tools, cars, and hardware stores, with his signature tagline, "Men are pigs"
>Starred in shows *Home Improvement* and *Last Man Standing;* played the title role in *The Santa Clause* and did the voice of Buzz Lightyear in the *Toy Story* films

WOODY ALLEN

WRITER AND DIRECTOR, NEW YORK CITY ♦ *Interviewed by Cal Fussman*

>**MY TWO TEENAGE GIRLS** think of me as ancient. But I'm up before them and wake them to go to school.

>**WHAT PEOPLE WHO DON'T WRITE DON'T UNDERSTAND** is that they think you make up the line consciously—but you don't. It proceeds from your unconscious. So it's the same surprise to you when it emerges as it is to the audience when the comic says it. I don't think of the joke and then say it. I say it and then realize what I've said. And I laugh at it, because I'm hearing it for the first time myself.

>**WITHOUT FEAR,** you'd never survive.

>**MY DAD DIDN'T EVEN TEACH** me how to shave—I learned that from a cabdriver. But the biggest lesson he imparted is that if you don't have your health, you have nothing. No matter how great things are going for you, if you have a toothache, if you have a sore throat, if you're nauseated, or, God forbid, you have some serious thing wrong with you—everything is ruined.

>**A CORNED-BEEF SANDWICH** would be sensational, or one of those big, fat frankfurters, you know, with the mustard. But I don't eat any of that stuff. I haven't had a frankfurter in, I would say, forty-five years. I don't eat enjoyable foods. I eat for my health.

>**MARSHALL MCLUHAN PREDICTED** books would become art objects at some point. He was right.

>**MY MOTHER TAUGHT ME A VALUE**—rigid discipline. My father didn't earn enough, and my mother took care of the money and the family, and she had no time for lightness. She always saw the glass a third full. She taught me to work and not to waste time.

>**I NEVER SEE A FRAME OF ANYTHING** I've done after I've done it. I don't even remember what's in the films. And if I'm on the treadmill and I'm surfing the channels and suddenly *Manhattan* or some other picture comes on, I go right past it. If I saw *Manhattan* again, I would only see the worst. I would say: *Oh, God, this is so embarrassing. I could have done this. I should have done that.* So I spare myself.

>**IN THE SHOWER,** with the hot water coming down, you've left the real world behind, and very frequently things open up for you. It's the change of venue, the unblocking the attempt to force the ideas that's crippling you when you're trying to write.

>**IF YOU'RE BORN WITH A GIFT,** to behave like it's an achievement is not right.

>**I LOVE MEL BROOKS.** And I've had wonderful times working with him. But I don't see any similarities between Mel and myself except, you know, we're both short Jews. That's where it ends. His style of humor is completely different. But Bob Hope? I'm practically a plagiarist.

>**WE TOOK A TOUR OF THE ACROPOLIS** late in the morning, and I looked down upon the theater and felt a connection. I mean, this is where Oedipus debuted. It's amazing for someone who's spent his life in show business or worked in dramatic art to look down at the theater where, thousands of years ago, guys like Mike Nichols and Stephen Sondheim and David Mamet were in togas, thinking, *Gee, I can't get this line to work.* You know, I've been working on it all night. And that actor, he doesn't know how to deliver it. Sophocles and Euripides and Aristophanes. *The costumes are late, and we gotta go on!*

>**IT'S BEEN SAID ABOUT MARRIAGE,** "You have to know how to fight." And I think there's some wisdom to that. People who live together get into arguments. When you're younger, those arguments tend to escalate, or there's not any wisdom that overrides the argument to keep in perspective. It tends to get out of hand. When you're older, you realize, *Well, this argument will pass. We don't agree, but this is not the end of the world.* Experience comes into play.

>**BACK WHEN I STARTED,** when I opened *Take the Money and Run*, the guys at United Artists accumulated the nation's criticisms into a pile this big and I read them all. Texas, Oklahoma, California, New England . . . That's when I realized that it's ridiculous. I mean, the guy in Tulsa thinks the picture's a masterpiece, and the guy in Vermont thinks it's the dumbest thing he's ever seen. Each guy writes intelligently. The whole thing was so pointless. So I abandoned ever, ever reading any criticisms again. Thanks to my mother, I haven't wasted any time dwelling on whether I'm brilliant or a fool. It's completely unprofitable to think about it.

>**YOU CAN ONLY DO SO MUCH,** and then you're at the mercy of fortune.

>**ME SITTING DOWN FOR DINNER** with Ingmar Bergman felt like a house painter sitting down with Picasso.

>**IT'S JUST AN ACCIDENT** that we happen to be on Earth, enjoying our silly little moments, distracting ourselves as often as possible so we don't have to really face up to the fact that, you know, we're just temporary people with a very short time in a universe that will eventually be completely gone. And everything that you value, whether it's Shakespeare, Beethoven, da Vinci, or whatever, will be gone. The earth will be gone. The sun will be gone. There'll be nothing. The best you can do to get through life is distraction. Love works as a distraction. And work works as a distraction. You can distract yourself a billion different ways. But the key is to distract yourself.

>**A GUY WILL SAY,** "Well, I make my luck." And the same guy walks down the street and a piano that's been hoisted drops on his head. The truth of the matter is your life is very much out of your control.

BIO   *BORN ALLAN STEWART KONIGSBERG, DECEMBER 1, 1935, NEW YORK CITY ♦ Interviewed June 3, 2013*

>Has written and directed nearly fifty feature length films in the last fifty years, including classics, *Manhattan*, *Annie Hall* and more recently *Midnight in Paris* and *Blue Jasmine*
>Nominated for twenty-four Oscars; has won four, including Best Director for *Annie Hall* in 1978
>Plays the clarinet

ANDRÉ 3000

MUSICIAN, ACTOR, DESIGNER, ATLANTA • *Interviewed by Cal Fussman*

>**MASTER** the mirror.

>**YOU'RE A SHIT.** *I love you anyway, but you're gonna have to correct that*. That's a friend.

>**KINGS ARE EXPECTED TO SLAUGHTER** and have different women. The pope: total opposite. So it's much harder to be pope than king. And on top of that, you've got to deal with the Sinéad O'Connors of the world.

>**YOUR VOICE IS BIGGER** in the shower.

>**IN AMERICAN MUSIC,** there's only eight notes. You can only flip them around so many ways.

>**THE REPETITION YOU HEAR** in hip-hop is addiction. It feels good, so you wanna keep doing it over and over and over again. Classical music takes you to all these places. Hip-hop is: *just keep that, just keep that, just keep that* . . .

>**I'M AN ONLY CHILD,** so I grew up to myself. I can't read a book in a room of crowded people.

>**NEVER LET YOUR RIGHT HAND** know what your left hand is doing. That came from my mom. She was saying you don't have to be so open and revealing to everybody—especially the people close to you.

>**WE DIDN'T HAVE BLOODS AND CRIPS IN ATLANTA.** In high school, it was fashion kind of gangs. How you dressed or danced was your crew. It was fighting but looking good while doing it. So there was this huge prep movement where ghetto kids were so into this world that Ralph Lauren had created that we were wearing riding boots to school. Benetton used to make these bags that were shaped to hold tennis rackets. We would wear them to school with a tennis racket inside, having never played tennis in our lives. Never! Those became the weapons in fighting—the tennis rackets.

>**OUR KIDS ARE SO OPPOSITE OF US.** When I was young, it was "I want new Jordans. I want Ralph Lauren and Polo." I try to buy my son new clothes and he says, "Naw, I'm fine. I'll just wear these until they tear up." He just doesn't care. And I love him for it.

>**ONSTAGE, YOU CAN HIDE** behind the music.

>**THE STUPIDEST ARGUMENT TO HAVE** with somebody is when you tell them what to like. How can somebody argue with you about what you like? "I want hot sauce." "Hot sauce? How can you like hot sauce?" Hey, it's *my* mouth.

>**I WAS A HARDCORE VEGAN** for fifteen years. I've even done raw. But socially it became horrible. I was kind of just sitting at home eating a salad. You become mean. That's not good for you.

>**SOMETIMES WHEN YOU'RE TRYING TOO HARD** to follow a rule, you're doing yourself more harm.

>**THE WORLD IS BIGGER NOW.** Your grandfather's grandfather's grandfather lived in one town, and maybe the girl he got was the only cute one in town. Hell, yeah, he's staying with her for the rest of his life! Made sense! But the environment has changed.

>**SEX IS REALLY LIKE BREATHING** or drinking a glass of water. We need to treat it as a normal thing.

>**THE PERSON WHO MOST IMPRESSED ME?** Prince. Michael Jackson was great. But Prince is *heavy*. When I say heavy, I mean encompassing an entire world instead of one feeling. Heavy is when someone's gonna give you their whole life—make you cry and smile. It's sexual. It's a commentary on the world. It's coming from a rawer place.

>**NUMBER ONE**—it's gotta have a great bed. But a great hotel for me means a great tub.

>**GROWING UP, *MENTOR* WAS NOT A WORD I KNEW.** I didn't know that word until five or six years ago. The way I explained the word to my kid is like this. I said: "Son, adults are really cool and I'll tell you why. Because you can compare them to a video game. If you played that video game for the last two years and you're proficient at it and I just jump on the game, you're quickly going to say: 'Hey, Dad, the trap is right there. When you get over there, you have to go, hop hop hop hop hop.' Now, if you didn't say that, it might take me a year to figure that out. So a mentor is: *I've done this, so I'm helping you get past that place*."

>**THE COMFORT ZONE** gets you nowhere—especially in music.

>**ONE THING I'VE NOTICED** about entertainers: Whatever's on the surface is an outcry for the opposite of what they're going through.

>**TRYING TO PLEASE** everyone is a stressful life.

>**WE FORGET THINGS** for our own protection.

>**BOREDOM KEEPS YOU GOING** because it makes you try to find ways to keep yourself exciting.

>**I DON'T LIKE TO GET OLD.** But the cool thing about aging is that the older you get, the harder it is to lie to yourself.

>**I HOPE I DON'T GET** hiccups no time soon.

BIO

BORN ANDRÉ LAUREN BENJAMIN, MAY 27, 1975, ATLANTA • Interviewed June 6, 2014

>Launched his career as one of the two members of OutKast
>Started a clothing line called Benjamin Bixby in 2008, which was resurrected as Bixby in 2012
>Played Jimi Hendrix in the 2014 biopic, *Jimi: All Is By My Side*

KEVIN BACON

ACTOR, NEW YORK CITY ◆ *Interviewed by Cal Fussman*

>BOB DYLAN told me never to drop a name.

>YOU DON'T WANT things to be nice and settled. You think you do. But you don't.

>THE REASON I'M LAUGHING IS because the first thing I was going to say was "Shut the fuck up and stay out of my way." But that's not really what makes a good director.

>BARRY LEVINSON is part of a very, very small club of directors who have hired me twice.

>WHEN THEY SAY, "That's a wrap," I kiss it good-bye. It's gone in a heartbeat.

>WHAT I GOT FROM MY FATHER was a burning desire to succeed. My father was into fame and leaving his mark. He was a city planner, sort of a genius in that world, the Robert Moses of Philadelphia. He was on the cover of *Time* once, and I remember going to his office and seeing, like, two hundred copies, which he would hand out to people. I would never do that in a million years. I don't save clippings. Anyway, we'd walk down the street, and even up to the time he died, people would say "Mr. Bacon," and I'd turn around and they'd be talking to him. What I got from my father, frankly, was the desire to be more famous than him.

>PEOPLE SEEMED amused by six degrees of separation, so why have a problem with it?

>IF YOU'RE REALLY MEANT to have a friendship, then it will sustain.

>YOU CAN'T LIVE BEHIND A GATE with an alarm on it, because you need to connect with people. They're the people that you're going to be asked to play. I play cops and assholes. Rarely do I get asked to play a movie star.

>*ANIMAL HOUSE* WAS MY FIRST MOVIE, so I didn't have anything to compare it to. I was a sight gag more than anything else. So I can't say it was one of those things where your life changes. When the movie came out, I had to ask for the night off at the bar. And I remember having a horrible time because nobody was recognizing me, and I went back to the bar to hang out for the rest of the night.

>THERE WAS A PRODUCTION OF *The Cherry Orchard* at Lincoln Center in the late seventies. My mother came up from Philly to see it with me. We're watching this play and it was incredible, and then the lights went out. It was a little awkward, because some people thought it was the end of the act. Eventually, Irene Worth, the star, came out and said, "There's been a blackout in all of Manhattan. And Brooklyn. And the Bronx. You'll be able to get your money back, but we're going to try to finish tonight's performance." The stagehands furiously tacked every single candle they could find onto the stage. They lit them all, and the ushers went to the front of the house with their flashlights and used them as follow spots. And they finished *The* fucking *Cherry Orchard*. It was one of the most beautiful things ever.

>*DINER* AFFECTED US in a cool way that none of us could see coming.

>STRESS, ANGER, and unspoken pain can really take a toll on your face.

>HOLLYWOOD IS more of an idea than a place.

>THERE'S THIS AMERICAN DREAM to put enough away that you can golf and build a birdhouse or just be in a Barcalounger watching football all day. I'll never be that guy. And I'm not really sure the people who have that are all that happy. Our desires as a man are to work, plow ahead, and overcome conflict.

>I'VE GOT DEAD FRIENDS who just didn't take care of themselves.

>THERE'S SO MUCH COMPETITION out there that being able to work at all is fucking amazing.

>REMEMBER WHEN we used to sit around and wonder, *What time is that show on?*

>YOU DREAM THAT AT A CERTAIN POINT you're going to be able to sit your kids down and give them this advice, and they're going to be looking at you like, "Please, tell me how to live my life." It doesn't really happen that way. Hopefully, they can absorb who you are.

>I DON'T THINK I'VE EVER FELT this much pressure in my life. I talk with some actors who say: "How many people watch is out of my hands. I can't control the audience response and the ratings and the digital downloads and all that stuff." I feel the opposite. I feel that it's all on me.

>THERE ARE A LOT OF THINGS I couldn't do before that I'll be able to do tomorrow.

>SOMETIMES I LOOK at the monitor after I've shot a scene and I go, *You're not that young, dude.*

BIO BORN JULY 8, 1958, PHILADEPHIA ◆ Interviewed September 27, 2013

>Played Jack Swigert in *Apollo 13*, Ren in *Footloose*, and Captain Jack Ross in *A Few Good Men*, along with nearly eighty other roles
>Plays guitar and sings in The Bacon Brothers, with his brother Michael
>Married to Kyra Sedgewick

TONY BENNETT

ENTERTAINER, NEW YORK CITY • *Interviewed by Cal Fussman*

>**I'VE BEEN VERY FORTUNATE.** I'm doing what I love and I'm getting away with it, you know?

>**FAME COMES AND GOES.** Longevity is the thing to aim for.

>**IF MUSIC SOUNDS DATED,** it means it wasn't very good in the first place.

>**MUSIC TEACHES** my painting and painting teaches my music.

>**I WAS SKETCHING IN A SLIT TRENCH,** hiding out, waiting for the Germans. All of a sudden, I heard a whistle. I knew immediately that it was coming right at us. The noise that it made was unbelievable. It overcame me. So I ran as fast as I could from that trench. I was twenty-five feet away when the shell hit exactly where I'd been sketching. What did it teach me? To be against war.

>**SING** like it's opening night.

>**NEVER OPEN WITH A CLOSER**—that comes from Count Basie.

>**EMERSON WROTE** how ignorant it is for people to be religious and say, *My God is better than yours*. That was 1841. We still haven't learned.

>**RESPECT** eliminates hate.

>**I DID A SHOW ONCE WITH LOUIS ARMSTRONG**—a television show. It was a hell of a show. All of a sudden, as Louis was playing, a fly landed on his nose. So he blew it off. He kept singing, and the fly came back on his nose. So he blew it off again. It was being taped, and everyone in the audience was holding their stomach, laughing. They didn't want to let their laughter out and ruin his performance. When Louis finished, everybody broke up. And then the director came out and said: "Let's do one more take without the fly." But that was the take they should've put on TV.

>**WHEN THE UNCREATIVE** tell the creative what to do, it stops being art.

>**WHEN I WAS STARTING OUT,** I used to stay onstage too long. Instead of criticizing me, Fred Astaire told me, "What I've learned is when you get a set together that's absolutely perfect, go in and pull out fifteen minutes of it." That was his way of telling me that less is more.

>**I CAN'T LIVE IN SAN FRANCISCO**—I'd never have an ounce of privacy. When I go to San Francisco, I know how the president feels.

>**JAZZ IS SO FABULOUS,** because you do the same song you did the night before differently than you did it the night before.

>**MY MOTHER WAS A DRESSMAKER.** We were very poor. But she said: "Always have a clean suit, a white shirt, and a black pair of pants and you'll be dressed."

>**YOU CAN** go anywhere in black and white.

>**ELLA FITZGERALD USED TO SAY** "We're all here." Three words. That really says it all. That's the way to treat people. "We're all here."

>**LUCK IS SOMETHING** that happens at the right time.

>**ANY GREAT PERFORMER** I've ever met has been frightened to go on.

>**IF THE ARTIST** doesn't give a shit, why should the audience?

>**I GOT THAT FROM A CABDRIVER YEARS AGO.** He said: "You singers, you're all losers compared to the singers I grew up with." I said: "How come?" He said: "Years ago, Al Jolson and Ethel Merman and people like them came out onstage and they hit the back of the house! They didn't have a microphone." He said: "You guys are faking it." So I said to myself: Let me try it. When I'm in an acoustical hall, let me sing a song at the end a cappella. At first, I didn't know what was gonna happen, but then I saw the reaction. This is good! So I left it in.

>**MY FATHER USED TO SING ON A MOUNTAIN IN ITALY,** and the whole valley would hear him. I have a photo of me singing "O Sole Mio" in the same exact spot. My son Danny was talking to some people and he came up with this idea: *What do you think of Tony and Lady Gaga singing "O Sole Mio" in Italian?* They went crazy. Having your kids involved in your career like that is very satisfying.

>**EVERYTHING OLD** becomes new again.

>**I'M NOT TRYING** to be bigger than anybody. My game is just to be one of the best.

>**I'M EIGHTY-EIGHT**—I have an awful lot to learn. My dream is to get better and better as I get older.

>**LATELY, I CAN'T BELIEVE IT.** I'm getting four or five standing ovations a night.

BIO *BORN ANTHONY BENEDETTO, AUGUST 3, 1926, NEW YORK CITY • Interviewed August 21, 2014*

>Served in the 63rd Infantry Division during WWII
>Discovered by Bob Hope in Greenwich Village in 1949
>Has sold over ten million records in the last ten years alone

JOE BIDEN

VICE-PRESIDENT, WASHINGTON, D.C. ◆ *Interviewed by Cal Fussman*

>**THE VICE-PRESIDENCY** is not a job designed to enhance your standing.

>**WHEN I GOT HERE IN '73,** the Democratic party was made up of a lot of old segregationists. So the idea that there was a united Democratic party, and that there was absolute civility, is a bit of a fiction. What was different then was more of a national ethic that you didn't publicly "trash" someone else. It was just bad form. But the feelings were equally as intense.

>**I KNOW IT SOUNDS CORNY,** but my definition of power is the ability to help people.

>**WHAT I HAVEN'T SEEN BEFORE IS** the intensity of the desire on the other side to see to it that Barack Obama is not president again. There seems to be a willingness to put that ahead of what might be a short-term—or a long-term—benefit to the American people.

>**MY DAD USED TO SAY,** "Without your word, you're not a man."

>**IT WAS 1957.** I remember because I was a freshman in high school. My parents seldom went out socially, but they went to the office Christmas party. My dad was the general manager of an automobile dealership. The owner was a wealthy man, and he was there along with the mechanics, salespeople, secretaries, and spouses. They had dinner, then cleared the tables for a band and some dancing. My mom and dad had told me they'd be back around midnight, but at about nine my dad walks straight into his bedroom. "What happened?" I asked. My mother said, "You know that promotion where you buy a car and get a bucket full of silver dollars? Well, the boss threw the silver dollars out in the middle of the dance floor for people to pick up. Your father turned to him and said, 'You can take this job. I quit.' " It's not like my father had an alternative. But that was my father. And my mother was proud of him.

>**NOBODY OWES YOU** a living. But everyone's entitled to dignity.

>**DOES IT FEEL LIKE HOME** or a thirty-three-room mansion? It feels like home for one reason: Every Tuesday, Wednesday, and Thursday night, one of my granddaughters comes and hangs out.

>**WHEN MY SON WAS A SENIOR,** I was asked to do a speech at Georgetown University. Father O'Donovan asked me to speak on how faith informs my public service. I'd never talked about my faith publicly. I mean, I acknowledge that I'm a practicing Catholic, but I don't think it's anybody's business, nor do I think it should matter to anyone. That's why I'm so angry about the way they treated Romney. Who I'm not crazy about, but...

>**ANYWAY, I NEVER WORKED SO HARD** on a speech my whole life. What I realized as I wrote it was the greatest sin a man or woman can commit is the abuse of power.

>**THE DECISIONS THE PRESIDENT MAKES** day in and day out are decisions that nobody sees. Trust me, if you had to make only one of those decisions, you'd be telling your grandchildren about it.

>**IT'S HARD TO FIND** a single project that everyone can see being created, like the Hoover Dam or the interstate highway system. The real answer is we need entire new industries.

>**THE FIRST DISCUSSION,** as we sat around this big table on the eightieth floor of some building in Chicago during the interregnum period, was with a group of about thirty economists. We weren't talking about *reorganizing* banks during that meeting. We were talking about banks going out of *business*. The action that the president took—and some of the antecedent actions on TARP—literally saved the economy from going off a cliff and the world going into a depression. Everyone forgets that now, especially our banker friends.

>**IT'S NOT A BAD THING** that people forget. My deceased wife used to say, "Joe, the greatest gift God gave to mankind was the ability to forget." To which my mother would always add, "If that *weren't* the case, women would only have one child."

>**AFTER MY FIRST WIFE AND DAUGHTER** were killed, my boys were banged up badly, and I had those aneurysms that didn't give me a big chance of living, my dad sent me a little three-paneled cartoon: *Hägar the Horrible*. I still have it on my desk. Hägar is in his Viking boat with his horn helmet, rowing away when a bolt of lightning comes out of the sky. Hägar gets charred. He looks up at heaven and says, "Why me, God?" And God comes back with "Why not?"

>**AS MY MOM WOULD SAY,** "Joey, as long as a person's alive, they have the obligation to strive. They're not dead until they've seen the face of God." So you just have to get your ass up—no matter what.

>**THERE WAS AN ARTICLE IN THE NEWSPAPER.** It said something like, "It's probable no vice-president has ever assumed the office with fewer assets than Vice-President Biden." I assume they were talking about financial assets.

>**MY DAD USED TO SAY,** "You know you're a success when you look at your kids and realize they turned out better than you." I am a success. But I should have had one Republican who wanted to be an investment banker and make a lot of money so that when they put me in a home, I get a window with a view.

BIO   *BORN NOVEMBER 20, 1942, SCRANTON, PENNSYLVANIA ◆ Interviewed October 25, 2011*

>Lost his first wife and baby daughter in a car accident before Christmas in 1972; his two sons were seriously injured
>He had a stutter as a child, but overcame the speech impediment by reciting Emerson and Yeats
>Served as a Delaware senator for 36 years; elected at the age of 29

DAVID BLAINE

MAGICIAN, NEW YORK CITY • *Interviewed by A.J. Jacobs*

>**MY LIFE IS SO BIZARRE,** it's just easier to be honest.

>**WHEN I WAS A KID,** I'd synchronize watches with my godfather, then tell him to call our house at a specified time during dinner. I'd be at the table and say, "The phone is about to ring." And he'd call and pretend he wasn't in on it. Then I'd play it up—I'd stare at the ceiling to make it seem like something weird was going on. All moms think their kids are special, but I wanted to make sure.

>**TO THIS DAY,** literally, I can't stop doing magic. Day and night. Like I just took a flight back from Italy last night. The whole flight was me doing magic for everybody—stewardesses, the captain, people in line for the bathroom...

>**I WAS SPOILED BY MY MOTHER.** Not in the sense that we had things. We didn't. But when I was with her, she never watched TV or talked on the phone. She was there. Reading books, going to museums, walking me through the park, bringing me to see guys playing the congas. All those things don't cost a penny, and yet I feel like I had the most incredible childhood.

>**YOU KNOW THE REAL REASON PEOPLE LIKE TO FAST?** Your brain functions at a much higher level. My thoughts, my memories, my creativity—it's pretty amazing.

>**YOU SHOULD ORDER ALL THE VITAMINS.** But not the multivitamins. Those are bullshit. Get the individual ones.

>**IT'S FUNNY,** because in my work I have extreme self-discipline, but in my life I have none.

>**WHEN I'M FUMBLING** and I'm not certain, really the outcome is set. It's misdirection. Athletes use it in the same way.

>**I ALWAYS USE THE FIRST URINAL** in the restroom. And sometimes I don't know which is the first urinal, so I'll start on the right one, then move to the left one. Then fuck it, I have to hit all of them.

>**WHEN I REALLY WANT SOMETHING,** I get obsessive over knocking on wood. I'll know that if I don't knock on wood, everything is going to fall apart. So I'll drive down the street on my motorcycle, and at every red light, I have to run off my bike, knock on that tree, that tree, that tree, and that tree before the light turns green.

>**NINETY-NINE PERCENT** of the people reading this will think I'm an insane person, but the 1 percent will understand.

>**MY MOM TAUGHT ME** not to be afraid of anything. Except for insects.

>**WHEN I ACTUALLY WAS BURIED ALIVE,** I learned that things aren't always as difficult as they seem to be.

>**OKAY, START WITH A PRETTY NEW DECK.** Secretly lick your finger. Have someone pick up half the deck and look at the card he cut to. As he's looking at the card, say, "Okay, put that half back on top." Point to the bottom deck and touch the top card with your wet finger. That'll act as an adhesive. The two cards will stick together. So he can cut as many times as he wants. When you spread out the cards, look for the two that are stuck together. His card will be the one on top of the one you touched with your wet finger.

>**WHEN I WAS WITH THE YANOMAMÖ INDIANS,** I counted four hundred mosquito bites on one arm. That was unbearable.

>**ONE LITTLE THING GOES WRONG**—like the guy who vacuumed the catheter tube when I was frozen in a block of ice—and then everything crumbles. You're having nightmares while your eyes are open. You don't know whether you're alive or dead.

>**WHEN I STOOD ON THE PILLAR,** I started to see people in trees. I thought the building behind me was shaped like a lion's head.

>**YEAH, THERE WERE WOMEN WHO FLASHED ME.** I forgot about that. It's not what you remember when you think of these things.

>**THE STRONGEST MAGIC IS IN PLANNING AHEAD.** I was set to do magic for George W. Bush, and I knew his Secret Service team was not going to trust a guy like me. So that morning, I found out where they were having breakfast in the hotel, and I did a bunch of effects for them. I made them feel comfortable. So when it came time to do magic for Bush, I was able to grab his wrist and steal his watch. I gave it back, but I didn't see any of them smiling this time.

>**BY THE WAY,** you should probably be having a minimum of 4.5 liters of water a day. It should never be cold. Just below room temperature. And you should probably have lemon in your water.

>**I WAS IN THE MIDDLE OF A DREAM** and when I opened my eyes, I looked around and thought I was floating in the ocean in a bottle. I realized I had to do it. I had to cross the Atlantic in a bottle. It became my obsession. I'm working with naval engineers to design a bottle that won't kill me.

>**MY HANDS ARE SMALLER THAN YOURS.** But they're delicate and fast. That helps.

>**A MNEMONIC DEVICE** needs to be bizarre. A lizard playing chess will stick in your brain. A fat woman sitting on a balloon.

>**IF YOU HOLD A LIT MATCH** at the top of a column of smoke, it will ignite the column and the flame will shoot down and reignite the wick.

BIO *BORN DAVID BLAINE WHITE, APRIL 4, 1973, NEW YORK CITY • Appeared in the August 2010 issue*

>Has lived 63 hours inside a block of ice, spent six weeks without food in a glass box suspended above the Thames, and stood on 20-foot pillar for 72 hours wearing chain mail while subjected to one million volts of electricity
>Held his breath for more than seventeen minutes in 2008, breaking the Guiness Record (a record that fell just six months later)

ALBERT BROOKS

ACTOR, DIRECTOR, LOS ANGELES ◆ *Interviewed by Cal Fussman*

>**I WAS ON** the defensive as soon as I got to the first class where they took roll. "Albert Einstein?" All the kids would be snickering. It's one of the three most famous names on the planet. You might as well be called Jesus Christ. Or Moses. First, I used the name Al, which I didn't like. But at least it sort of camouflaged it. The thing is, I liked the name Albert. I just couldn't use it with Einstein. So I changed the last name when I thought I could really accomplish something, and I didn't need that name to be funny.

>**WHEN THEY MADE** *90210*, there were people outside of Beverly Hills who went, *Oooooh!* But you don't go *Oooooh!* when you're in there. You're worried about passing the Spanish test.

>**IN THE BEGINNING** of any career, in every job, people are always forcing you to the middle.

>**I'M NOT** a person who I ever thought would do well with divorce. Not that it can't happen. I just didn't want that. So I waited a long time to meet the right person. Then I finally met someone that I was willing to be divorced from.

>**ART AND RESISTANCE** are great together. That's what art's made for. Look at Vincent van Gogh: He didn't cut off his ear because he was selling well.

>**ACCEPTANCE IS** going to a restaurant where the salad's not great, but the steak is fine.

>**THE BIGGEST WASTE** of brainpower is to want to change something that's not changeable.

>**RELAXATION** is the absence of worry.

>**I WAS ON** the road opening for Neil Diamond in the early seventies. That was a reasonable audience. Better than opening for Sly and the Family Stone, that's for sure. When the headliner got a little more hard rock and the drugs became heavier, it wasn't a good mix for comedy. Ever try and be funny to a guy on meth?

>**ALL YOU HAVE TO DO** to be a bad guy in a movie is put a knife into somebody's eye. But when you look at the real bad guys in the world, they're all people you'd have a drink with. Ted Bundy was the most personable guy in the world. John Wayne Gacy was a fucking clown at a party.

>**I'VE NEVER** been disappointed, because I've never given somebody I liked that much power.

>**I DON'T KNOW** that I can define fear. But one of the sources of fear is holding up some sort of model life that doesn't exist and feeling like you're far away from it.

>**YOU CAN EQUATE** acting to a tennis game: When you're playing one of the best, you get better.

>**I HAVE CHILDREN.** I have a family to support. But I really could live in a one-room apartment, as long as the television worked. I never needed anything. Just a comfortable chair and I'm fine.

>**THERE'S NOTHING** funny about flying to Houston.

>**A LOT OF PEOPLE** say they'd like to be a billionaire. But they never ask themselves: *Do I want the brain of that billionaire?* They think about the money. But to have that money, you'd need that kind of brain, and you'd have to have those thoughts at night and all the stuff that goes with it.

>**SO I THINK** if you're happy with your brain, you're powerful.

>**MY FATHER** died at a huge Friars banquet in 1958. It was for Lucille Ball and Desi Arnaz. He got up in the middle of the show, came to the mic, and just killed. You can hear Desi laughing—I have this on tape. It was always amazing to me how it happened. He didn't die on the way to the mic. He didn't die in the middle. He was great, and he finished. Then he sat down and died. He had a lot of bad commas along the way, but he had a great period.

>**MY MOTHER** was supportive without knowing it. Deep down she wanted all the right things, she just didn't see the world like I did, and she's not supposed to.

>**LOOK,** I was never Elvis. I held myself back. I turned things down. I made it very difficult for myself to become famous, and maybe it was so I could process it all. But it's gone on gradually over a long time, and I don't have paparazzi following me.

>**I GOT SO GOOD** at writing to a budget, my brain was restricting myself. I'd write, "It's a stormy night." Then I'd cross out "stormy." I'd write: "It's a calm night." Then I'd cross out "night". It's noon. Because you know how much night costs. You know how much rain costs. Nothing comes free in movies.

>**I HAVE TRIED** to tell an original story to my kids every night of their lives. I must've told five thousand stories. When I try to repeat one three years later, my daughter says, "You told that one." Kids have the opposite of Alzheimer's: They remember too much.

>**WE'RE AN ODD** animal that understands there's an end. My dog doesn't know she's going to die. She can't. If she knew she was going to die, she would know how to drive.

BIO
ALBERT LAWRENCE EINSTEIN, BORN JULY 22, 1947, BEVERLY HILLS ◆ *Interviewed September 30, 2010*

>Studied drama at Carnegie Mellon University
>Started his career as a stand-up comic, appearing on *The Dean Martin Show* and *The Ed Sullivan Show*, before acting in his first film, Martin Scorsese's *Taxi Driver* in 1976
> Did the voices of supervillian Hank Scorpio and Jacques the bowling instructor on *The Simpsons*

JAMES L. BROOKS

WRITER AND DIRECTOR, LOS ANGELES • *Interviewed by Cal Fussman*

>THERE'S A REASON there's a reason.

>I ALWAYS FIGHT hard to push a movie to the point where it pulls me.

>EVERY LAUGH you have at the keyboard does not mean everybody else will laugh. But laughing helps sustain you to move forward.

>*THE SIMPSONS* has a dynamic of its own not quite controlled by anybody. This is a show that will follow anybody doing any kind of comedy. You could do broad comedy, romantic comedy, farce, social commentary, satire. You could do burlesque. Everybody serves the show. And the Simpsons stand ready in their dressing rooms.

>MY FATHER was an alcoholic and model of what to avoid. My mother taught me survival.

>LINKING up the things you were with the things you become is what growing up is.

>I HAD AN ARGUMENT years and years ago with another comedy writer. Jack Nicholson and Dustin Hoffman were the biggest guns at the time—long may they wave—and we had an argument about which one was number one. I took Jack, and I finally won the argument by saying he could play either role in *The Odd Couple*.

>I HAVE A RULE in research: The third time you hear something, it's generally true.

>AM I CONSTANTLY surprised when things work out differently than I'd expect? Sometimes. Sometimes the surprise isn't pleasant and you want to blow your head off.

>I HAVE SALESMAN'S BLOOD, and unfortunately I exist in a time when everyone's a salesman.

>THE DIFFERENCE between sex and love? Well, the great thing is when there isn't one, right?

>NOTHING'S going back to the way it was.

>YOU'RE NOT GOING to hear with a straight face about a guy that doesn't participate in child care anymore. It just doesn't exist. That thing that people made movies about—*Mr. Mom*—is about as antique as any notion of fatherhood could be right now.

>THERE'S ALWAYS something falling to the floor. I'm a juggler in constant oops mode. Every day. There are days when my laughs are pretty hollow. Dust comes out of your mouth and your bones make a funny sound. But I'm laughing.

>TO ME, every script should begin with, "Fade in: Tax-incentive state." That's what happens.

>THAT FIRST PROMO tour: "*Oh, my God*. Somebody's meeting us at the plane." "*Holy shit*. There's a limo." By the third stop it's "Where's the limo?"

>*THE MARY TYLER MOORE SHOW* came along at the beginning of the women's movement. I don't think that show was seminal. I think its timing was seminal.

>A TELEVISION JOB that's working is the best job in the world. You get to do something you like. You get to do it with people you like— usually. You have community of a sort that you're denied in movies, because shows can go on five, seven years, even decades. People meet, they get married, they have children. It's like a town. It's enormously secure—until it isn't. But as long as it is, it is, and it's great.

>EVERY DAY, somebody talks to me about Albert Brooks.

>IN THE MOVIE I have coming out, the heroine has a saying taped on her mirror: "Courage is mastery of fear, not absence of fear."

>IN THE HISTORY of the earth, there's never been more people writing. Everyone's a writer. Everybody spends time trying to let people know who they are. Twitter.

>NOTHING IS a matter of course when you get to do your own thing. It's always a gift that can stop giving and probably will.

>TWICE IN MY LIFETIME magazines have done surveys on the best character on television: One recently was Homer, which was great. The other—at the time—was Danny. It's just insane what that meant. Danny DeVito beat out Jackie Gleason. That's fantastic. *Taxi* wouldn't have happened without Danny. His was the home run, and nobody else could've gotten to first base with that character.

>PEOPLE ALWAYS marvel at this gossamer thing that happens in life, and it happens often enough, so we all get to hope for it.

>WHENEVER she walks in, and it's the right she, you're lucky.

>I SAW *Annie Hall* with a group of people working in comedy and television. We were all stunned. Stunned. It was like watching a spaceship land. That something that funny could also be that beautiful.

>YOU KNOW you're in love when you're more yourself than you ever imagined possible. I put that line in the movie, but then I had to cut it out. Maybe I'll get it back in there. I'm still working.

>YOU ROOT for your son to have a girl he laughs with.

BIO BORN MAY 9, 1940, NORTH BERGEN, NEW JERSEY • *Interviewed October 15, 2010*

>Co-created *The Mary Tyler Moore Show, Taxi, The Simpsons*; wrote, produced and directed the classics *Terms of Endearment* and *Broadcast News*

>Has won twenty Emmys and three Oscars

JIM BROWN

ATHLETE, ACTOR, OHIO • *Interviewed by Cal Fussman*

>PEOPLE SAY I'm seventy-two years young. My ass. I'm seventy-two years *old*. But you've got to live to get old. You can't get old without living.

>I'M NOT a Martin Luther King and a Gandhi motherfucker. I don't know what they were talking about. Spit on my ass and I'll knock you out. I ain't going to sing and march, man. But I'm fair.

>IF YOU TRULY believe something, and it's incorrect, that doesn't mean you don't have integrity.

>THE GREAT WARRIORS have sensitivity because the dedication to giving your life up for a cause is sensitive as hell.

>A BULLY is a coward.

>THE HEISMAN TROPHY couldn't be my issue. I didn't win the Heisman Trophy because blacks couldn't win it back then. But that didn't stop me. My performance, my dedication, my hard work is the issue. I'm sitting here because I'm one of the hardest working cats that ever lived. I won over the American public with my performance.

>YOU AIN'T SETTING NO EXAMPLE calling upon religious symbols. Just do the right shit. Treat people good, man. Show up on time. Be honest.

>WHEN YOU GET OLD, you realize how fragile kids are. So delicate, man. Any little shit that gets in their brain can fuck them up. They need order.

>DON'T GET HOSTILE and don't call nobody out. Just have the question and ask why.

>A LIBERAL IS arrogant enough to think he can do you a half-assed favor. He is superior enough to think he can give you something that you don't deserve. A liberal will cut off your leg so he can hand you a crutch.

>YOU CAN'T help a motherfucker sitting on his ass, crying the blues.

>YOU CANNOT get me to be disloyal to a friend. You just can't do it. Loyalty is a part of what I live by. I didn't say I was going to be loyal to my friend because he was right. I'm going to be loyal to my friend because he's my friend.

>TO LEAVE at twenty-nine years old, MVP, having won the championship in '64 and played for it in '65. To go into the movies and break the color barrier and be in a sex scene with Raquel Welch. To get to be in *The Dirty Dozen* with some great actors. To make more money in one year than you damn near made in nine years of football. Everything about it was ingenious.

>I GAVE AWAY most of my trophies, put away the plaques.

>GOD AIN'T got nothing to do with winning a damn football game.

>SEX IS always wonderful, but it's like having a great meal. It is only what it is. It can never be everything in itself. And it has a downside that's devastating. When you understand sex, you understand that your fidelity is the greatest thing you have. It's yours, not hers.

>THE NEED to be cared for is the base of everything. In the penitentiaries, you won't hear gangbangers and criminals say, "No, I don't want to be cared for by nobody." When you care about them, they'll open up to you. They'll tell you shit they'd never tell for money or for sex.

>IT'S THE BIGGEST CRUTCH we can ever have: *I'm a victim because of what white folks did. I was a slave. I didn't get a fair shot when I went for the job that they didn't give to me.* I look and say, *Look how you look, motherfucker. I wouldn't hire you myself.* So let's deal with the fundamentals, man. Get yourself together and then we can fight the battle.

>TELL YOU WHAT you got to do to compete. What you got to do to compete is compete.

>YOU GOT THE TRICKLE-DOWN EFFECT. But what if I live in Watts? Poor people, you can vote a hundred times a day, you ain't gonna get that shit.

>ULTIMATELY, the soil replenishes.

>IF YOU'RE SMARTER THAN ME, tell me some shit. I'll listen, you know. This is an open forum.

BIO

BORN FEBRUARY 17, 1936, ST. SIMMONS, GEORGIA • Interviewed August 2, 2008

>Qualified for the Olympics as a decathlete in 1956, but declined to compete so he could concentrate on football
>Never missed a game in his nine seasons with the Cleveland Browns
>After his football career, became an actor and starred in *The Dirty Dozen* and *100 Rifles*

JAMES LEE BURKE

NOVELIST, MISSOULA, MONTANA • *Interviewed by Cal Fussman*

>THERE'S NO SUCH THING as bad food in south Louisiana. It's on a level with heroin.

>MY FATHER USED TO SAY, "If everybody agrees on it, it's wrong." Or, as Dave Robicheaux, the protagonist in some of my books, says, "Did you ever see a mob rush across town to do a good deed?"

>THE BOOS always come from the cheap seats.

>I WAS TEACHING BACK IN THE SIXTIES. I remember a lot of kids had this in-your-face attitude, as though it were a testimony to liberation from convention. Well, there's a reason for convention. We use signals to people to indicate emotions that we can't verbally state or express. There's a reason you take off your hat when you walk into somebody's house.

>IF YOU LEARN ANYTHING WITH AGE, it's that ultimately you don't solve the great mysteries. I don't know why the good suffer. I'm a believer, but I don't understand the nature of God. I don't understand the nature of evil. I sometimes look around and think maybe we're not gonna make it as a species. I sometimes wonder if there isn't some active force that is intent on destroying the earth.

>DEEP-FRIED CRAWFISH has got enough cholesterol in it to clog a sewer main.

>PEARL AND I MET IN A GRADUATE SEMINAR, British Romantic Poetry. She didn't have a textbook. I lent her mine. We'll be married fifty-three years in January.

>MAYBE THERE ARE YOUNGER PEOPLE TODAY who find it's just easier to dissolve a marriage rather than work through the problem, but I'm not judging them for that. I mean, it's better than waking up with someone's throat cut.

>THERE'S NO substitute for loyalty.

>RESPECT INVOLVES ACCEPTING PEOPLE for what they are without revising or marginalizing or objectifying them—or even elevating them.

>THE GREAT LINES are in the dialogue that's around us all the time; it's just a matter of hearing it.

>WE GAIN no wisdom by imposing our way on others.

>MY BOOK *The Lost Get-Back Boogie* was rejected 111 times before it was eventually published by Louisiana State University Press. When you get thoroughly rejected—and I mean thoroughly rejected—you realize you do it for the love of the work. And you stay out of the consequences. I developed one rule for myself: Never leave a manuscript at home more than thirty-six hours. Everything stays under submission. Never accept defeat.

>EVERY GUY WHO COVERS THE POLICE BEAT knows the reality of what goes on in these southern police stations. You learn this as a reporter: If you ever see in a police story written in the passive voice, "The subject was subdued," that means he got a baton upside the head or he was thrown down an iron fire escape.

>PEOPLE TALK ABOUT THE VIOLENCE IN MY WORK. I've never written anything that I don't believe I can defend. The last couple of books in the Dave Robicheaux series deal with the abduction and the abuse of women. Those things happened. And part of the theme of the books was the indifference toward the deaths of these women. They were all killed in one little area, about sixty miles from New Iberia, and that's the point. Everyone thinks it's just something a crime writer made up. No. It happened. There was just no news follow-up at all on the deaths of these young girls. They were all marginalized people.

>LET ME TELL YOU SOMETHING ABOUT VIOLENCE: I turn on cable TV, and the stuff I see there is unbelievable. I can't even watch it.

>AMERICA IS THE MOST CREATIVE PLACE on Earth because of the dynamic mix of ethnicity and cultural backgrounds, and the tensions those create. Tension is always created by opposition. Standardization is the enemy of invention.

>MY WIFE IS CHINESE, and she says one of the surviving graces of the Chinese peasantry, the working class, was always their sense of humor. I knew that, even as a child, about people of color. They had this great sense of humor; otherwise they wouldn't have survived. It's an irony that the people who laugh the most are those who have suffered the most.

>A TIME THAT I WRITE WELL but briefly is when I'm really tired. Because that's when things come out naturally. The problem is I just can't stay with it. Fifteen or twenty minutes of that and I'm shot.

>IF I LEARNED any truths in life, it's this simple: It's family and friends. That's it.

>I HAVE TO ADMIT I laugh a lot while I'm writing. I just don't know that anyone laughs with me.

BIO *BORN DECEMBER 5, 1936, HOUSTON • Interviewed October 25, 2012*

>Has written nearly three dozen crime novels. His second book, *The Lost Get-Back Boogie*, was short-listed for the Pulitzer in 1978
>Has also worked as an oilman, a land surveyor, and a social worker

GEORGE H. W. BUSH AND BARBARA BUSH

FORMER PRESIDENT AND FIRST LADY, KENNEBUNKPORT, MAINE • *Interviewed by A.J. Jacobs*

>**GEORGE H. W. BUSH:** Dad led by example. Mother would lecture us.

>**SHE'D SAY,** *Give the other guy credit. Nobody likes a braggadocio, George. Don't talk about yourself all the time.*

>**DAD WOULD JUST GO OUT** and do stuff. He would come home from Wall Street on the train. The other men would all go home and have a dry martini. He'd go down and serve as the moderator of the Greenwich Representative Town Meeting. And we remembered that.

>**OH YEAH, I HAVE A PIECE** of the Berlin Wall . . . they make them in San Antonio.

>**WHAT STRUCK ME** about her? Her beauty. Her sheer beauty. And her dress! She had on a green-and-red dress. Spectacularly beautiful woman. And I asked somebody, *Who is that beautiful girl?* "That is Barbara Pierce, why?" I said, *Well, I'd like to meet her.* And he brought her over. We said hi. Then they started playing a waltz. I said, *Barbara, I don't know how to waltz.* And she said, *Well, let's sit down.* So we sat down, and the rest is history. Been sitting down for sixty-five years.

>**NEVER DID** learn to waltz.

>**BARBARA BUSH:** I think you ought to treat your spouse like you treat your friends. You clean your house for your friends, you make sure they're taken care of, and a spouse comes second. I think you oughtta treat him like a friend.

>**GB:** It's been pretty easy. You might not know this, but Bar's not that difficult to live with.

>**BB:** If you each go 75 percent of the way, it's a perfect match.

>**GB:** I waited till my eighteenth birthday to sign up. My dad wanted me to wait two more years. But he was all for it.

>**BB:** He was proud of you. I think that was the only time you ever saw your father cry.

>**GB:** He took me down to the station to say good-bye. And off I went. Knew nobody in the navy. It was different then. Most everybody wanted to serve.

>**I WAS WALKING** out of the high school chapel at Andover. And somebody came running across campus and said there's been an attack. The next day, December 8, they convened a special chapel service. The headmaster, a tough guy, said, "All right, when you hear that 'Star-Spangled Banner' played, I want to see you guys standing at attention! I don't want you slouching in here like you've done here all the time." Never forgotten it.

>**I WENT BACK** to Chichi-Jima in 2001. They said, *This is where your plane went down.* It was very emotional for me. You go to this little town and there are all these Japanese kids with flags—"Welcome, welcome."

>**I DON'T REMEMBER** a lot of the details. Also, I think of my mother—"Nobody likes a braggadocio, George." I'd rather sit and look at the surf out there. So beautiful.

>**I WAS OFFERED A JOB** on Wall Street by my uncle. But I wanted to get out. Make-it-on-my-own kinda thing.

>**BB:** You told me that you sat on the subway and realized you wanted to work with something you could touch, not Wall Street.

>**GB:** Well, I don't remember that. But I could well have said that back then.

>**THE USS GEORGE H. W. BUSH** is a great thing in my life. It's amazing. A great honor. The difference between this and the old carriers when I was a pilot is unbelievable. Five thousand people on it—it's like a city.

>**GORBACHEV WAS ALWAYS** very pleasant. I was the first one to have any contact with him, because I went over as vice-president when he took office. And so I told Reagan that we've got a different guy here, a different leader. He's easy to work with, good sense of humor. Could be tough, he could get angry; but I liked working with him. I give him great credit for how the world is today.

>**I WENT TO SEE** Lyndon Johnson, and I was telling him I wanted to run for Senate. And he said, "The difference between the Senate and the House is the difference between chicken salad and chicken shit." Johnson was amazing.

>**WHEN I WAS PRESIDENT,** trying to rally the country behind what became Desert Storm, Jimmy Carter wrote all the members of the United Nations Security Council and urged them not to support me in the resolution that would have given all countries, really, the right to use quote whatever means necessary unquote, and aggression. That means use force. And he lobbied against it. He went to foreign leaders. I mean it's just unconscionable. They asked him about it last night on the TV.

>**TIDDLYWINKS** is a very important game. We haven't played lately, Barb. The secret—it's the wrist action. It's a delicate flip with the . . . it's hard to explain.

>**MOST RESTAURANTS WE GO,** they remember—you're the one that doesn't like broccoli. You gotta be famous for something.

>**WELL, THE WORST THING** about the time that I was president I think was losing the election. Yeah, I really wanted to win, and I read smart reporters saying all these harsh things, like "He's not really trying" and "He feels he's got it." And that's not really true at all in my view. So that was a hurtful thing.

>**I LOVED GOING** to Camp David. That was a marvelous getaway. You get on a helicopter, you're up there in twenty-eight minutes from the White House lawn. You get off the chopper and there's no press, no nothing, you just go in and see the top-run movies. You could talk to foreign leaders without intrusion.

>**I DIDN'T GIVE** him any advice at all. But I was a very proud dad.

>**BB:** Too late, if he hadn't learned by then. He had a good example.

>**GB:** I never said, *Now that you're president, here's what you've gotta do*—no advice like that. He had his own people around him, good people. I had my chance.

>**THE GREAT THING** about *Air Force One* is when you go to some foreign country, it's kind of the symbol of the United States. People are pointing it out and . . . magnificent aircraft. Magnificent.

>**BB:** Compare it to the Russian one we were on.

>**GB:** Well, that was old and awkward.

>**BB:** Dark and dreary.

>**GB:** But we don't wanna criticize because we were lucky to be on it.

>**THE QUEEN'S BEDROOM** was good. That's where we stayed when George was president. There was kind of a wicker thing over the toilet in the Queen's Bedroom. There I was, sitting where Barbra Streisand had sat. I couldn't believe it!

>**BB:** Cut that, George.

>**GB:** Why? What's wrong with that?

>**I LOVED** "Hail to the Chief." Loved it. Not like Jimmy Carter.

>**BB:** He thought it was too much folderol.

>**GB:** What did I think my kids would do?

>**BB:** We thought that they would be dictators.

>**GB:** No, we didn't know.

>**BB:** We just prayed they'd grow up.

>**GB:** They were all wonderful and we were very blessed.

>**THEY ARE.**

>**I GOT PRETTY GOOD** at horseshoes. I got to be family champion here for a while.

>**I THINK THE PHRASE** "kinder and gentler" resonated. I don't remember how I came up with it. Probably some speechwriter wrote it. But I felt that way. Still do.

>**IT'S MUCH WORSE** to read criticism about your son than yourself.

>**BB:** He read every word.

>**GB:** Read it. Listened to it.

>**I LOVE THE PHRASE** "insurmountable opportunities."

BIO   *BORN GEORGE HERBERT WALKER BUSH, JUNE 12, 1924, MILTON, MASSACHUSETTS* • *Interviewed September 20, 2010*

>Flew 58 combat missions and earned a Distinguished Flying Cross for service as a torpedo bomber pilot during WWII
>Served as a congressman, an ambassador, and director of the CIA before becoming president in 1988

BIO   *BORN BARBARA PIERCE, JUNE 8, 1925, NEW YORK CITY*

>Met George Sr. at a dance at the Round Hill Country Club in Greenwich, Connecticut, in 1941. They married in 1945
>During the 1940s she worked at a nuts and bolts supply factory that supplied the U.S. war effort
>Has been an ardent supporter of finding the cure for leukemia ever since her daughter died from it as a toddler

MICHAEL CAINE

ACTOR, LEATHERHEAD, ENGLAND • *Interviewed by Cal Fussman*

>**NOBODY IMPERSONATED ME** when I was a child. Where I came from, everybody talked just like me.

>**I'M COCKNEY,** which is a certain type of working-class London. We are all funny—all of us. I've never met a Cockney who wasn't funny. We do not have a miserable side. But we do have a ferocious side. Someone once asked, "Do Cockneys commit suicide?" I said, "No. If they get pissed off, they murder people."

>**YES, THERE IS A BEST LESSON** my mother taught me! There is! It was during the Second World War. I was six and my brother was three. When my father left to join the fight my mother was crying, and then she pulled herself together and turned to the two of us, and instead of saying, "Oh, I've got to look after the two of you, and I'm on my own," she said: "Your father's gone. Now you two have got to look after me." And we went, "Right, mum. Don't worry. We'll do that. We'll take care of you. It's okay." And she made men of us with one sentence.

>**POVERTY TAUGHT ME** not to worry about money.

>**ACTORS, WHAT DO WE DO?** We study behavior. I never went to drama school. I learned my acting on the subway, watching how people moved and what they did.

>**THE GREATEST COMPLIMENT I EVER RECEIVED** came while I was working with Sir Lawrence Olivier. Lord Olivier. We were making a film called *Sleuth*, and I did a scene with him. When it finished, he looked at me and said, "I thought I had an assistant. I see I have a partner."

>**NEVER WEAR ANYTHING** to make people look at you.

>**IN THE RESTAURANT,** my wife always says, "You didn't look at the bill." I say, "I don't want to worry myself by looking at the bill and asking, *Who had the onion rings?* or *They overcharged me for chips*. Because those moments all add up to years. And how much money would you pay for another year?

>**I WAS MAKING A MOVIE IN THE PHILIPPINES:** *Too Late the Hero*. It's a war story, in the jungle, with the Japanese. And I was at this big, very posh party in Manila. Everybody started introducing me, and then, finally, the hostess, who didn't speak very good English, came up to me and said, "Are you a drug dealer?" I said, "No. Why do you ask?" She said, "Well, why does everybody call you, 'My cocaine?'" That's a true story! I'm not smart enough to invent that, you know?

>**I HAD COME TO HOLLYWOOD** to star in a picture called *Gambit*. I used to sit in the lobby of the Beverly Hills Hotel and look out for film stars. One day, John Wayne came in, saw me, and said: "Are you in that movie called *Alfie*?" I said, "Yeah." He said, "I just saw that. It's very good, son." And we became friends. He gave me some advice. He said, "Never wear suede shoes." I asked why, and he said, "Because you'll be taking a piss in a men's room, and there'll be a guy next to you, and all of a sudden the guy will recognize you, and he'll turn and go, 'Michael Caine!' And he'll piss all over your shoes!" I never wore suede shoes again.

>**I SEE A FROG** and think it's not really worth killing their whole body for just those little legs.

>**YOU KNOW WHO SAVED MY LIFE?** Tony Curtis. I was at a party. This was when Tony Curtis was very famous. I knew who he was but had never met him. I was speaking to someone by a fireplace and took the end of the cigarette that was in my mouth, lit another cigarette with it and went on talking and smoking. Then I felt a hand come around behind me and go into my pocket. Tony Curtis took the cigarettes out and threw them in the fire. He said, "You don't know me, but I've been watching you. That is, what, the fifth cigarette you've lit in less than an hour?" He said, "You're gonna die. I've just saved your life for you." He was right. You can't smoke cigarettes like that and live. And I stopped.

>**FATIGUE DOESN'T HAPPEN** until you suddenly go, "I'm bored."

>**ONE RULE OF PARENTING?** Forgive everything.

>**THERE'S SO MUCH MEDICINE.** So many advances . . . My friend Quincy Jones always says to me, "If you live another five years, they'll discover so many things, you'll live another five."

>**YES, YOUR FEARS DO DIMINISH** with age—'cause your memory goes and you forget what you're afraid of!

>**YOU COULDN'T TELL IF I WAS LYING.** But I could tell if you were.

BIO   *BORN MAURICE JOSEPH MICKLEWHITE, MARCH 14, 1933, LONDON • Interviewed August 4, 2014*

>Has played lead in over 75 films
>Won two Oscars for his performances in *Hannah and Her Sisters* in 1986 *and* The Cider House Rules *in 1999*
>Keeps a 21-acre garden on his estate

CHEVY CHASE

ACTOR, BEDFORD, NEW YORK • *Interview by Cal Fussman*

>**MARGE** is a terrible name for a mistress.

>**MY FATHER WAS** the funniest guy I ever met. I'm not sure if I stole his stuff or if I inherited it. My stepfather was a psychoanalyst. You might think he'd have known better than to hit kids.

>**YOU COULD KNOCK MY TEETH OUT** and break my nose and there'd be something funny about it to me.

>**BILLY MURRAY AND I** came to fisticuffs, but we never really ended up hitting each other. We tried, but Belushi got in the middle and we both ended up hitting John. And if anybody deserved to be slapped in the forehead it was John, for instigating it all.

>**THE BEST ADVICE** I can give you about falling is to never land.

>**I NEVER SHOT THINGS UP** or freebased. I was pretty low-level when it came to drug abuse. I checked myself into the Betty Ford Clinic after my nose started to hurt.

>**LOVE IS HUGE.** But if you're talking about men and women, it's got to start with the most initial obvious attraction that warthogs go through. Look at that ass! That's what keeps the world spinning. There's your God.

>**I'M STILL IN LOVE** with my wife the way I was when I fell in love with her thirty years ago. That's luck.

>**HOW MUCH MORE** do you have to write about Jonah and the whale and that poor guy with pimples—Job! Good reading, but it all comes down to the golden rule: Do unto others . . .

>**MY FAVORITE FOOD IS EGGS.** I like 'em over easy on a muffin with a little ham. I can have four of those every morning. I eat more eggs than anyone I know. How can you not love eggs? It's our birthright.

>**I WENT TO COLLEGE** with every intention of being a doctor. I was redirected by my grades. That, and a fake radio show that I improvised with some friends. Wasn't even on the air.

>**I DON'T THINK EGGS** are so filled with cholesterol as people think. The problem comes in with how they're made, the sauces and that kind of stuff. I could be wrong.

>**I REMEMBER** the first "Update" I did on *Saturday Night Live*. They had big cameras back then, and you were looking into a huge lens. I wasn't nervous at all because I looked right through that lens and imagined the faces of the seven funniest people I knew. It never occurred to me that millions of people were watching. What I did was just for the eight of us.

>**IT TAKES** somebody smart to play somebody dumb.

>**IT'S ALL TIMING**—Nixon leaving. Ford handed the presidency. Luckily for me, Ford kept on tripping over things. I didn't make any attempt to do an impression of him. I would simply take a nice fall or hit my head out of nowhere and get huge laughs for it. People used to joke that it really hurt Ford in the election he lost to Carter. It was close, and someone said I got a point in the New York primary.

>**I LEFT *SATURDAY NIGHT LIVE*** after that first year. I never wanted to work for more than a year on anything.

>**WHAT MAKES A HOME, HOME?** Animals and a little bit of clutter.

>**I WISH JOHN WERE ALIVE TODAY.** I'd love to see. Would he have kids? Would he be a grandfather? What would he look like? What you realize is, there aren't that many funny people in the world. You lose a guy like Belushi . . . ah, it's hideous.

>**CHILDREN FORCE YOU** to grow.

>**MICHAEL O'DONOGHUE WAS** a great writer and thinker. He's the guy who put the line on the *National Lampoon*: "If you don't buy this magazine, we'll kill this dog." He had a line that summed it up. But you have to understand that Laraine Newman had the biggest honker. After a year or two, she left the show and had her nose done. She looks great. It's now a normal nose. Not that big nose that we all knew. One day, I was at Michael's house and he was commiserating. He said, "We've lost John. We've lost Gilda. We've lost Laraine's nose."

>**IT WILL EVENTUALLY BE** discovered that the more you sleep, the healthier you are. Which means you'll really be at your healthiest when you pass away.

>**A GOOD NAME** for a mistress would be close to a man's name so that nobody would know. Like . . . Conane.

>**THERE'S NO VACATION** from being a parent.

>**I ALWAYS FLY FIRST CLASS.** To remind myself.

>**LIVE A LIFE OF GRACE.** You'll be a better person for it and so will your children.

>**BREAK AS FEW BONES** as possible and make as much noise as you can.

BIO
BORN CORNELIUS CRANE CHASE, OCTOBER 8, 1943, NEW YORK CITY • *Interviewed January 20, 2010*

>Part of the original cast of *Saturday Night Live*
>Once sustained a groin injury impersonating Gerald Ford that kept him off the show for two weeks
>Notable films: *Caddyshack*, *Fletch*, and *National Lampoon's Vacation*; other notable TV role: Pierce Hawthorne in the cult hit, *Community*

CHRIS CHRISTIE

GOVERNOR, TRENTON, NEW JERSEY • *Interviewed by Scott Raab*

>GROWING UP, IF WE WERE having an argument, my mother thought that was great. At least we were talking.

>EVERYTHING OUT ON THE TABLE. You're not happy today? I wanna know why. Let's fix it and move on. I got that from my mother.

>ALL THE BEST MANAGERS in baseball were catchers.

>I CAUGHT A GUY IN HIGH SCHOOL who went on to play pro ball. His father was this quiet retired Marine drill sergeant. This kid threw a ninety-four-, ninety-five-mile-an-hour fastball. But he also had a good curveball. Freshman year one game, we made a guy look silly on two curveballs in a row—strike one, strike two. I called a third curveball. The kid hit it about 350 feet. That night I went to my friend's house for dinner. And his father said to me in his quiet way, "Chris, let me ask you something. That third curveball: I couldn't see from where I was standing. Did you call it or did Scott shake you off to the curveball?" And I said, "No, I called it." And he put his fork down on his plate—I can close my eyes and still see this guy doing this—and he said to me, "Don't ever do that again."

>IF YOU'RE GONNA get beat, get beat on your best pitch.

>I HAVE SO MANY IDEAS I want to talk about, but if you talk about too many, no one's going to hear you.

>I THINK I'M MUCH FUNNIER reacting to people than I am just coming out and telling jokes. I have fun going back and forth. That's the atmosphere I lived in. Sitting around that kitchen table having dinner, you better be on your game. Because the conversation was fast and it was sharp, and if you wanted to be at the big-persons' table, you had to keep pace.

>VERY RARELY DO I HAVE SECOND THOUGHTS about something I said. But one time I would have dialed it back was with the Navy SEAL at one of our town-hall meetings. I let him speak, I was trying to answer, but he kept interrupting me. And he told me he was a law student. So I told him, *If you conduct yourself in court like that, you're gonna get your rear end thrown in jail by a judge.* Now, I should have stopped right there. But then I said, "Idiot." He was acting like an idiot, but if I had the chance, I would have just ended it at telling him not to interrupt.

>EVERY ONCE IN A WHILE, you go a little too far.

>YOU HAVE TO BE ABLE TO PERFORM ACTS OF KINDNESS to show people that you have it in you, but you also better be able to show people your tough side. If you don't, they'll try to walk all over you.

>I WOULD NEVER DO WELL in a legislature. I would be too frustrated.

>I AM FROM HERE, and I am this place.

>I WAS IN THE CAR COMING HOME from a dinner the night I found out Clarence Clemons died. And I turned to Mary Pat and I said, "My youth is over." Because that's what Bruce and his band represents to me: It was my youth. It was my teenage years, my growing up, my college years—they represent that to me. You come to terms with the fact that you're getting older.

>LAST SATURDAY, I brought my first child to college. That night I was putting my twelve-year-old son to bed, and as I was tucking him in, he said to me, "Dad, do you miss Andrew?" And I said, "Sure." I said, "Do you?" And he said—this is a twelve-year-old—he said, "More than I have words to describe." Whew. So I tucked him into bed, and I said, "Well, listen, if you need to talk, you know you can talk to Dad." And he said, "Sure. You're my man." And I go to walk out of the room and close the door, and he said, "Dad, come here for a sec." So I came back in, and he said to me, "And Dad, if you need anything tonight, I'll be right here."

>I FEEL CARICATURED at times as the Jersey guy, the fat guy. Sure. But I understand that if you're a public figure, that's what's going to happen. It's amazing how thick your skin gets—quickly.

>MY WIFE SAYS TO ME, "Why did you make our son a Mets fan? You coulda let him be a Yankee fan and he coulda been happy." I said, "As a Mets fan, he's going to understand pain and disappointment. Other losses that he experiences in life, he'll keep in perspective." You don't change your loyalty.

>I WANT PEOPLE TO WALK AWAY every time they see me and say, That guy's really appreciative that we gave him a chance to do this job.

>I DON'T ANSWER HYPOTHETICAL QUESTIONS as a general rule. They keep asking them, though.

BIO | *BORN SEPTEMBER 6, 1962, NEWARK, NEW JERSEY • Interviewed September 11, 2012*

>Ordered New Jersey state buildings to fly their flags at half-mast when actor James Gandolfini died

>Chilly relationship with idol Bruce Springsteen thawed after Hurricane Sandy. "We hugged," Christie said. "He told me, 'It's official. We're friends.'"

FRANCIS FORD COPPOLA

DIRECTOR, NAPA, CALIFORNIA • *Interviewed by Stephen Garrett*

>**WHEN I WAS SIXTEEN OR SEVENTEEN,** I wanted to be a writer. I wanted to be a playwright. But everything I wrote, I thought, was weak. And I can remember falling asleep in tears because I had no talent the way I wanted to have.

>**DID YOU EVER SEE** *Rushmore*? I was just like that kid.

>**I'VE HAD WINE** at the table all my life. Even kids were allowed to have it. We used to put ginger ale or lemon soda in it.

>**I DID SOMETHING** terrible to my father. When I was twelve or thirteen, I had a job at Western Union. And when the telegram came over on a long strip, you would cut it and glue it on the paper and deliver it on a bicycle. And I knew the name of the head of Paramount Pictures' music department—Louis Lipstone. So I wrote, "Dear Mr. Coppola: We have selected you to write a score. Please return to L.A. immediately to begin the assignment. Sincerely, Louis Lipstone." And I glued it and I delivered it. And my father was so happy. And then I had to tell him that it was fake. He was totally furious. In those days, kids got hit. With the belt. I know why I did it: I wanted him to get that telegram. We do things for good reasons that are bad.

>**PEOPLE FEEL** the worst film I made was *Jack*. But to this day, when I get checks from old movies I've made, *Jack* is one of the biggest ones. No one knows that. If people hate the movie, they hate the movie. I just wanted to work with Robin Williams.

>**I WAS NEVER SLOPPY** with other people's money. Only my own. Because I figure, well, you can be.

>**TEN OR FIFTEEN YEARS** after *Apocalypse Now*, I was in England in a hotel, and I watched the beginning of it and ultimately ended up watching the whole movie. And it wasn't as weird as I thought. It had, in a way, widened what people would tolerate in a movie.

>**I SAW THIS BIN** full of, basically, garbage film. We had shot five cameras when the jets came and dropped the napalm. You had to roll them all at the same time, so there was a lot of this leader, which was just footage. So I picked something out of this barrel and put it in the Moviola and it was very abstract, and every once in a while you saw this helicopter skid. And then over in sound there was all this Doors music, and in it was something called "The End." And I said, "Hey, wouldn't it be funny if we started the movie with 'The End'?"

>**I HAVE MORE** of a vivid imagination than I have talent. I cook up ideas. It's just a characteristic.

>**I JUST ADMIRE** people like Woody Allen, who every year writes an original screenplay. It's astonishing. I always wished that I could do that.

>**TO DO GOOD** is to be abundant—that's my tendency. If I cook a meal, I cook too much and have too many things. I was just watching a Cecil B. DeMille picture last night based on Cleopatra, and I realized how many parts of the real story he left out. So much of the art of film is to do less. To aspire to do less.

>**WHEN I WAS STARTING OUT,** I got a job writing a script for Bill Cosby. He used to have the very best wine for his friends. He didn't drink wine himself, but he had this wine called Romanée-Conti, which is considered one of the greatest wines in the world. I never knew wine could taste like that. He also taught me how to play baccarat. And one night I had $400, and I won $30,000. So I bought $30,000 worth of Romanée wines.

>**YOU HAVE TO VIEW** things in the context of your life expectancy.

>**THE ENDING WAS CLEAR** and Michael has corrupted himself—it was over. So I didn't understand why they wanted to make another *Godfather*.

>**I SAID,** "What I will do is help you develop a story. And I'll find a director and produce it." They said, "Well, who's the director?" And I said, "Young guy, Martin Scorsese." They said, "Absolutely not!" He was just starting out.

>**THE ONLY THING** they really argued with me about was calling it *Godfather Part II*. It was always *Son of the Wolfman* or *The Wolfman Returns* or something. They thought that audiences would find it confusing. It was ironic, because that started the whole numbers thing. I started a lot of things.

>**I WAS IN MY TRAILER,** working on *Godfather II* or *III* in New York, and there was a knock on the door. The guy working with me said that John Gotti would like to meet Mr. Coppola. And I said, "It's not possible, I'm in the middle of something." There's an old wives' tale about vampires—that you have to invite them in, but once they cross the threshold, then they're in. But if you say you don't want to meet them, then they can't come in. They can't know you.

>**I NEVER SAW** *The Sopranos*. I'm not interested in the mob.

>**WHAT GREATER SNUB** can you get than that absolutely nobody went to see *Youth Without Youth*? Anything better than that is a success.

>**SOME AUDIENCES** love to sit there and see all the names in the credits. Are they looking for a relative?

>**WHAT SHOULD I DO NOW?** I could do something a little more ambitious. Or less. Better less. For me, less ambitious is more ambitious.

BIO BORN APRIL 7, 1939, DETROIT • *Appeared in the August 2009 issue*

>Has directed over twenty-five films, including *The Godfather* trilogy and *Apocalypse Now*, and won six Academy Awards
>Owns the Francis Ford Coppola winery
>One of its products: a canned sparkling wine named for his daughter Sophia

KEVIN COSTNER

ACTOR, SANTA BARBARA, CALIFORNIA • *Interviewed by Cal Fussman*

>**YOU CAN LEARN** a lot more by what a man does than by what he says. I just watched how my father did things. He worked for the Southern California Edison company, and often when it stormed, the lines would go down. The phone would ring at two in the morning. And my mom, knowing that he'd been out working for two straight nights, would tell him, "I can say you're not back yet." And he'd say, "No, hand me the phone."

>**IF YOU WANT A JOB,** and you're not as good as the next guy, then work longer than the next guy. Work faster. Be there before him—because talented people show up late, and sometimes shit needs to get done.

>**I WAS PRETTY GOOD** in school until algebra—when the numbers turned negative. I could never grasp that. I knew how to add and subtract. I knew how to divide the cookies in the tree house so that things were fair. But I couldn't get negative numbers. I got left behind and lost a lot of confidence because of it. On a certain level, I don't know if I ever did turn that around.

>**PEOPLE SEE ME** as very successful now. They aren't willing to put my life in reverse. They don't want to know that on the construction site I had to choose between the Ding Dongs and the chocolate milk. Every day the lunch truck came by when I was framing houses. I wanted the chocolate milk. But it cost more than the plain milk. So if I chose the chocolate milk, I didn't have enough money to get the Ding Dongs. If I have one carryover from those days, it's about food and having to choose based on money. Somebody I'm dining with will look at the menu and not be sure which of two entrées to order, and I'll say, "Why don't you try them both?"

>**I NEVER USED** a negative number in my whole life. I doubt you have, either.

>**IF SIX EXECUTIVES** read something, and the rumor going around town is it's not very good, then no one thinks it's good. If I think something's good, I don't fall out of love with it.

>**REMEMBER THE DAYS** when you could only see *The Wizard of Oz* or *It's a Wonderful Life* once a year? When you see a movie that is incredibly crafted, you see something new every time you see it.

>*HOW THE WEST WAS WON* was very important to me. It was a four-hour movie. I didn't think it was too long. I didn't think it was long *enough*. I didn't leave my seat during intermission because the overture was playing.

>**I DON'T LIKE DEFINITIONS.** I like four-hour movies.

>**I LIKE THE FAT** in life, not just the lean storytelling. I think the fat gets you through the winter. I love subplot. I love extra rabbit holes you can go down. Sometimes, if we give things time, they reveal themselves to us. Look, everyone has sat around the campfire and seen somebody talk too long and not get to the point, and there's this silent humph. But there are other people who talk around that campfire, and right at the end of their story it all ties together. And you think, *My God, that was a story! And I needed to go to every place the storyteller took me to get the full impact.*

>**AT THE END OF THE DAY,** *Waterworld* was a bargain. A lot of money was made off that movie. A lot. But after all that's been written, who's going to believe that?

>**IF YOU'RE GOING** to tear down a hero, you should never forget that you're tearing down someone else's hero. You're tearing down somebody else's son. You might have to face her one day.

>**YOU'VE GOT TO UNDERSTAND.** I'm a public-school guy. Sometimes you have to push somebody up against a chain-link fence if you feel they've done you wrong.

>**SEE THAT JACUZZI** over there? I used to sit in that Jacuzzi at night and look out at those oil rigs in the ocean. I'd look at those oil rigs, but I didn't see oil rigs. I saw an armada. Knowing that tomorrow they're going to land and we're going to have to fight.

>**I'M IN A POSITION** where whatever I do, I can get my head handed to me. I'm in a position to fail because there is a whole group of people out there who want me to fail. It's a weird vibe.

>**WHO DOES HE THINK HE IS?** *Like he's going to clean up the ocean.* Hey, number one, I'm not saying I'm going to clean up the ocean. What I am saying is I have an absolute tool that can effectively separate oil from water.

>**YOU HAVE TO TRY** to dismiss the loudness of cynicism. It's certainly going to come.

>**YOUR DAD KNOWS EVERYTHING.** Then, somewhere along the line, you inherit that manner. Your kids think you know everything. And everybody ends up with this deep, dark secret that there are so many things you don't know.

>**I KNOW WHAT I KNOW** and it's not enough. I know that when I die, I'm going to miss a lot of great books and a lot of great music that I'll never hear. I'm going to miss seeing my children's children. I'll miss boyfriends and husbands who I'm going to be absolutely dependent on to treat my children with respect and grace, and take care of them and honor them. That's what I'm going to miss.

>**FRESH WATER** is everything.

BIO BORN JANUARY 18, 1955, LYNWOOD, CALIFORNIA • *Interviewed February 2, 2012*

>Best known for roles in *Bull Durham* and *Field of Dreams*, but his first sports movie was *American Flyers*, a 1985 cycling film
>Founded the company Ocean Therapy Solutions, creating a high-speed centrifuge that separates water from oil, which was sent to help clean up the Gulf of Mexico after the 2010 BP oil spill

WILLEM DAFOE

ACTOR, NEW YORK CITY ◆ *Interviewed by Cal Fussman*

>**THERE'S A REAL WISDOM** to not saying a thing.

>**TURN OFF THE SOUND** in a movie, and if you can tell what's going on, the movie should work.

> **"DON'T SPIT ON YOUR LUCK."** My wife always says that. Good Italian woman. It's like a mantra for her.

>**SPITTING ON TOM CRUISE** in *Born on the Fourth of July* was pretty much fun if I remember right. Not to be taken personally, certainly.

>**MY FATHER USED TO SAY,** "You don't deserve it if you can't take care of it." I've always been haunted by that.

>**LET'S SAY YOU'RE A REALLY BOORISH PICKUP ARTIST.** Certain phrases aren't available to you in a foreign country, because you don't have the language available to you. So you have to put a kind of new sincerity into these little phrases. Maybe that's why some men do better in other countries.

>**CORRUPTION IS SOMETHING** you face all the time. Avoid it.

>**I HAVE NO DOUBT** that if I met Bob Dylan, it would be disappointing—and annoying to him. But that's why I like Bob Dylan.

>**I WAS REALLY LUCKY.** The father of a friend of mine had tickets and he said to his son, "Who do you want to invite along?" That's how I got to go to the Ice Bowl. I felt really guilty. I was a Green Bay Packers fan, but I was twelve years old and there were people who would have killed for that ticket. I was so worried about being cold that I put on so many socks that I think I cut off the circulation in my feet. I must've gotten frostbite. When I got home, my feet were screaming pain. Only in retrospect do you appreciate how fantastic that game was.

>**YOU GOTTA LEAVE WISCONSIN** behind when you're playing Christ, right?

>**I THINK YOU DO YOUR BEST WHEN** you're doing it for someone else. Think of when you're first in love, what power that gives you. You're like Superman—because you're doing it for someone else.

>**BEFORE WE STARTED FILMING** *Platoon,* we had these Vietnam veterans take us out in the bush, and for two weeks, with no contact to the outside world, they taught us how to do soldierly things . . . It was beautifully practical, and it created a special stake. We wanted to respect their experience. You always have to earn your right to pretend.

>**AT SOME POINT** when I do a role, I feel like I'm the only guy to do it. Nobody else should be doing this. You always gotta get to that place where you own it.

>**OF COURSE THE DEVIL COULD TEMPT ME.** What he could offer me would be that state where you disappear into an action. When you disappear into doing. It's the sensation that I seek over and over again. When you're in motion and doing something and the world drops away and you become that thing. I would take that if I could sustain that forever.

>**IF YOU CALL IT A RISK,** it's probably not a risk.

>**I WAS BORN WILLIAM,** but I was called Billy growing up. I didn't like it. It was diminutive—it didn't have any force to it. So as a kid I was always looking for a nickname. It doesn't take a psychologist to tell you that would be a form of mask.

>**WHEN I WENT TO MILWAUKEE,** I was living in this house with a bunch of crazy people, and one guy really took it upon himself to call me Willem. *Willem.* And it kind of stuck. When I became an actor, I thought of changing my name back to William, but that seemed too formal and British. So I just stayed with Willem and now go through life with a fake name.

>**I REMEMBER THE FIRST TIME** I saw my name on a marquee. I was in Hong Kong. *To Live and Die in L.A.* I never thought I cared about those things, but it was exciting. Probably because it was in Hong Kong.

>**WHY DO I DIE SO MUCH?** It's confusing to me. Maybe it's because I like strong characters. And it's natural that in a story sometimes they want to get rid of those strong characters.

>**CELEBRITY IS OKAY** as long as you know it's not about you.

>**THE THINGS THAT YOU WORRY ABOUT** aren't the things you should worry about. The things that you don't worry about are the things you should worry about.

>**SOMETIMES THERE** is no second or third take.

>**IT'S NEVER ONE OR THE OTHER.** It's always that balance between control and abandon. How much control, and how much do you let it go? You're always regulating between the two.

>**AS I GET OLDER,** I die less.

BIO *BORN WILLIAM DAFOE, JULY 22, 1955, APPLETON, WISCONSIN* ◆ *Interviewed November 18, 2011*

>Son of a surgeon and one of seven brothers and sisters
>Has worked on films with Wes Anderson, Lars Von Trier, and Martin Scorsese
>Performed most of his own stunts as the Green Goblin in the *Spider Man* films

DANGER MOUSE

MUSICIAN, LOS ANGELES • *Interviewed by Cal Fussman*

>**SOMEBODY CAN SAY THAT THEY LOVE YOU,** but the really important thing is whether you actually believe it.

>**I DON'T WANT TO KNOW THE RULES.** I'll just do what I do and I can always pay people who know the rules to come in and tidy things up.

>**WHEN I WAS YOUNG I NEVER THOUGHT OF MAKING MUSIC.** I didn't realize it was art. I just thought it was entertainment, and I didn't want to be an entertainer.

>**I WENT TO THE UNIVERSITY OF GEORGIA AS A BUSINESS MAJOR.** But the people I befriended were into art and music and films and we started going to see some bands. The music would be really good and they'd do things that were really strange and weird. The music never got played on the radio. And I didn't understand. I thought the whole point was to try to be famous on the radio, and I didn't have a desire to do that myself. So when I started to understand that music could be art and you can make your own choices, I thought: *Well, I don't have to know how to play anything. I can just make stuff.* I sold some of my books and used my loan money to start buying instruments and ways to record in my dorm room. Right away I got into making music by any means.

>**THINGS THAT ARE WORTHWHILE** take a while.

>**THERE WAS THIS MOMENT.** I was in a bar playing pool and I heard this song that I hadn't heard before and I just sat and listened and listened and listened. It was so beautiful with this long, big guitar part. And then I went up to the bartender and asked, "What is this song?" He just kind of looked at me like *You don't know?* It was Pink Floyd. "Shine On You Crazy Diamond." From an album that was ironically released the year that I was born. And I thought to myself, Okay. I've heard the name Pink Floyd. I've seen it on T-shirts. I assumed it was a loud rock 'n' roll band that I just didn't care about because it wouldn't have been cool for me in high school to listen to Pink Floyd. But this music just blew me away. And a thought hit me, *How many other things have I been missing because it wouldn't have fit in with me socially?* The next day I turned in my hip-hop stuff and got every Pink Floyd CD I could.

>**THAT MOMENT CHANGED THE WAY I SAW THE WORLD.** What food had I not eaten because it looked a certain way? What people had I not hung out with because they dressed differently?

>**WHEN I WAS A DJ** I tried to come up with a name that didn't sound like I was taking myself too seriously. *Danger Mouse* . . .

>**CERTAIN THINGS YOU SAMPLE WON'T SOUND GOOD** if you play them over and over. They'll just get annoying. Certain things, if the chords are right and it feels a certain way, you can loop it and it'll sound good for three minutes.

>**WHEN BANDS THAT START OUT SMALL** get bigger, there's a big thing that gets lost. It's almost like the early fans feel like somebody's just slept with their girlfriend, like their girlfriend's out there just sleeping with everybody now and it's just ruined it, you know? They feel hurt. And I feel that way with my own records, like my record has just become a real floozy, a fast girl out there just tearing it up. I lose a certain amount of intimacy with my own records after they're out there with everybody.

>**I WAS ALWAYS TERRIFIED ON STAGE.** I'd have nightmares about it. Usually I'll start counting my mistakes really early on. It's a way to distract myself that there are thousands of people watching. Once I get to ten I stop counting.

>**YOU CAN HAVE A MEDIOCRE MELODY** and a great lyric, and it can work. And a great melody with a mediocre lyric. But one of those has to be really, really strong.

>**IT'S THE RELATIONSHIPS** I wound up having with the people I've worked with that have made me be able to have an actual career out of this if you call it a career. I still don't know what the hell I'm doing, really . . .

>**I WANT TO HEAR EVERY SONG THAT I COULD EVER LOVE.** That could take awhile. I'm still working on it.

BIO   *BORN BRIAN BURTON, JULY 29, 1977, WHITE PLAINS, NEW YORK* • *Interviewed November 11, 2014*

>Made a name for himself with *The Grey Album*, an unauthorized mash-up of the Beatles' *White Album* and Jay-Z's *Black Album* in 2004
>He has since collaborated with James Mercer in Broken Bells and Cee Lo Green in Gnarls Barkley and has produced U2, Black Keys, and others

CHARLIE DANIELS

MUSICIAN, NORTH CAROLINA • *Interviewed by Scott Raab*

>**I GOT NO AXES** to grind and nothing to hide. Anything you want to talk to me about, please do. You will not offend me, I promise you.

>**I AM VERY PRO-LIFE.** I am very pro-family. I am very pro-God. I very much believe in what I write and what I say.

>**I DON'T LIKE** the terminology Left/Right, Republican/Democrat, because you're swinging an awful wide loop there, and you're liable to catch some people in it you don't want to.

>**TIME IS** too important, too precious to spend in dissension. I despise arguing. I can get along with anybody in the world if they give me a chance to. If I can't get along with them, I just won't go around them. I try to live in peace with people. I was probably on my way to learning anyway, but I'm sure having the prostate cancer fortified my view to some extent.

>**I'M HAVING** a colonoscopy every two years. I call him the cable guy.

>**I GOT EVERYTHING FROM BEETHOVEN TO BILL MONROE** on my iPod. Charlie Parker—I'm a big Charlie Parker fan. Oh gosh, yeah. How could you not be? What a genius the man was.

>**FIRST TIME I HEARD ELVIS PRESLEY,** I hated him. He was on the Ernest Tubb Midnight Jamboree and he sang Blue Moon of Kentucky, and I'm a big bluegrass fan, and I thought, *Man, you are murdering that* song. My *gosh*, don't do that. But he changed it all. He made it possible for a country boy to play rockin' music.

>**I DON'T THINK** Elvis was Richard Burton, but I think his acting capabilities were way past what they ever gave him to do. I think he could've done more.

>**I WORKED** at a creosote plant. I had a bunch of black workmates, and they kept talking about Randy's Record Shop, and I had no idea what they were talking about. I come to find out what it was was WLAC in Nashville—late at night, they would go to what they called "blues radio." I was living in North Carolina, but the station came in at night like a local station, and these black guys used to listen to it all the time. It was a whole 'nother world out there that we had never been exposed to.

>**MY DAD** knew more about a pine tree than anybody I've ever met.

>**YOU OWE THEM** a show regardless of how many of them it is, or if you've had a fight with your wife, or you have a hangover. When you start forgetting that, those people don't show up the next time you come to town.

>**I TRY,** I *really* try, to entertain people.

>**I LOVE** playing golf—I don't want to spend my life doing it. I love riding horses—I don't want to spend my life doing it. I love fishing, but if I fished all the time, I'd get tired of it.

>**FORTY-FOUR YEARS.** Marry somebody you love. That's the whole thing. And continue to love them. Keep your attention at home.

>**IT DEPENDS ON WHAT YOU CALL SUCCESS.** Success to me is to be happy. As far as success in your work is concerned, it's to do a caliber of stuff that you're not going to be ashamed of. We all do stuff that we're not 100 percent happy with, but still and all, do something that you can kind of be proud of.

>**I DON'T LIKE** renting stuff. I like to own stuff. I like ownership. We own both buses and the truck.

>**EVERY TIME** I get a dog, something happens to it. We live out in the country, and you raise dogs in the country, they don't know anything about cars, and they'll run up under one. I had one dog that got snakebit, and I've had a couple three run over. So I just decided, till I could stay home more, there's no sense having a dog.

> **"THAT LONESOME** whippoor-will, he sounds too blue to fly, the midnight train is whining low, I'm so lonesome I could cry." Shakespeare never said it any better. But you can like Hank Williams and you can still like Shakespeare.

>**THE ONLY PLACES** you can get a decent piece of barbecued brisket is Texas, Oklahoma, or Kansas.

>**YOU EVER EAT** barbecued bologna? In Oklahoma, I guess they put it on a spit. They gash it and they brush it with sauce and cook it—it's really good. They put a roll of it on. It's very good. Oh, you must try it sometime.

>**IF I HAVEN'T** learned it by now, I'm never going to learn it.

BIO BORN OCTOBER 28, 1936, WILMINGTON, NORTH CAROLINA • *Interviewed September 12, 2008*

>Played bass on three Bob Dylan albums
>Won a Grammy for his hit "The Devil Went Down to Georgia" in 1979
>Inducted into the Grand Ole Opry in 2008

TED DANSON

ACTOR, LOS ANGELES ◆ *Interviewed by Cal Fussman*

>**A FRIEND IS** someone who will allow me to be a really bad friend and not hold it against me.

>**MY LESSONS** didn't come at my father's knee. Like all good lessons, they were learned from example.

>**I GREW UP** in Flagstaff, Arizona, without a television or any connection with pop culture. My father was a director of a museum and research center. Many of my friends were Hopi kids, which meant I'd go to their villages and mesas. They'd pray and dance to their gods the way they'd been doing for hundreds of years. So I was blessed with tolerance.

>**COURAGE IS** something I don't know how much I have. You can't plan for it. You either do the right thing or you don't when the moment comes.

>**COMEDY HAS** to be rooted in sadness or it's worthless to me. Sam Malone, the alcoholic . . .

>**IF YOU'VE GOT INTEGRITY,** it will smack you very hard when you fuck up.

>**IF YOU DON'T HAVE INTEGRITY,** you'll go on for a very long time beating the crap out of people, robbing, stealing—and there's nothing inside you that tells you what you're doing is wrong. Life won't even bother to slap you.

>**TO GROW UP** knowing you're loved is astounding. It's a huge gift to a child.

>**THE ONLY REASON** to be a celebrity is you get to meet interesting people.

>**YOU WANT TO KNOW** who you are in the world for real? Hang around with your kids. They don't give a rat's ass what you do for a living.

>**THE SECRET** to our marriage? We laugh a lot.

>**YOUR KID** turning sixteen is a reason for prayer. As a parent, they're out of your control. You never had control anyway. But now it's really clear that you need to pray—because that's all you've got.

>**A GOOD SCRIPT** is one that doesn't let you go, "I get it!" on page 5.

>**MY WIFE** has known Bill and Hillary Clinton for thirty years. Bill is like her big brother. It's not so much the president part that strikes you about him, as he is so remarkably bright. They're both so powerfully bright. Their great joy in life, the thing that bonds them together, is that they love to fix things. It's just a joy to be around them. We laugh and talk about kids and life and movies—it's not what you'd think.

>**ANYTHING GREAT** can be used as a weapon.

>**WHEN YOU'RE NOT** in love and you've just had sex, then it's kind of like, "Well, what's next?"

>**EVERYTHING** that I thought or believed in went flying out the window in the face of the stark realness of my mother dying. I really have no idea. . . .

>**WE COULD** commercially fish out the oceans while at the same time environmental damage messed with the bottom of the food chain. There are so many stresses on the ocean that we could literally collapse it if we're not careful.

>**LOOK,** no one gets out of this alive. That's not the game plan. We all die. So nobody's going to get an award for saving the planet and get to live forever. Okay, then, let's engage the problems with a joyous and hopeful heart. Because it doesn't matter if we blow it. It's not like this is a desperate game where if we win, we won't die. We all die.

>**WHY IS IT** that we can make our sandwiches together, walk our dogs together, roll up our sleeves and make something in our community better, but as soon as we talk about ideas, whether it's religious or political, we become entrenched. I can't stand what looks to me like the selfish, shortsighted righteous far Right. They cannot stand my liberal dada dada. And we will fight to the death. When only two minutes ago we were making sandwiches together.

>**CAN I HAVE** as many guests as I'd like? Okay. Three. Jesus of Nazareth. Muhammad. And Buddha. We'd have some grape leaves—something simple and easy to digest. A little green tea. I'd say, "Fellas, let's talk . . ."

>**TO BE HELD** in low esteem by Larry David is like being on Nixon's enemies list.

>**YOUR CHILDREN** may rat on you. Your wife will fire back at you. But if you're not kind to your dogs, what can they do? A really big test of how kind a human being is comes with how well he treats his dogs.

>**ACTING WAS** the perfect outlet for a guy like me, who's always wondering what it's like to be you.

BIO BORN DECEMBER 29, 1947, SAN DIEGO ◆ *Interviewed September 14, 2010*

>Won two Emmys for his star turn as Sam Malone on *Cheers*; more recently appeared in *Bored to Death, Damages,* and *Curb Your Enthusiasm*
>Helped create the American Oceans Campaign in 1987, now known as Oceana
>Has also written a book called *Oceana*

ROBERT DE NIRO

ICON, NEW YORK CITY ◆ *Interviewed by Cal Fussman*

>**THOSE WHO SAY** don't know. Those who know, don't say. That holds up over time.

>**SO DOES:** If you don't go, you'll never know. I tell that to my kids.

>**TEN YEARS** seems only a few years ago.

>**IF IT'S THE RIGHT CHAIR,** it doesn't take too long to get comfortable in it.

>**ITALY HAS CHANGED.** But Rome is Rome.

>**WE MADE A RUBBER WALL** for the jail scene in *Raging Bull*. It was hard rubber foam. Smashing your head into a real wall wouldn't have been possible. You've got to do it till you're happy.

>**I'D LIKE TO LOOK** at all of my movies once just to do it—just to see what it makes me think, to see what the pattern was. But with all the movies I've been in, that would mean watching two or three a day for a month. I don't know where I'd get the time.

>**IF MARTY WANTED** me to do something, I would consider it very seriously even if I wasn't interested.

>**MY DEFINITION** of a good hotel is a place I'd stay at.

>**IF I REMEMBER** correctly, there were not many sequels at the time. *The Godfather* was one of the first. So we didn't think about sequels the way we do now. I remember seeing the entire street between Avenue A and Avenue B converted into the early twentieth century. The storefronts, the insides of the stores. The size of it was incredible. You knew what you were doing was ambitious.

>**I'LL ALWAYS BE** indebted to Francis.

>**WHEN I DID** *THE DEER HUNTER*, I thought, Thailand is such an interesting place. I'll be back soon. But I didn't get back for something like eighteen years.

>**YOU SHOULD'VE DONE THIS.** You should stand up for this more than that. The president's got to deal with that every moment. Imagine what it would be like with all the different forces coming at you, having to compromise, to weigh the consequences of one decision as opposed to another. It's tricky. Come to think of it, it's kind of like being a director.

>**I ALWAYS TELL ACTORS** when they go in for an audition: Don't be afraid to do what your instincts tell you. You may not get the part, but people will take notice.

>**FROM JODIE FOSTER:**

By the time I got the role in Taxi Driver, I'd already made more stuff than De Niro or Martin Scorsese. I'd been working from the time I was three years old. So even though I was only twelve, I felt like I was the veteran there.

De Niro took me aside before we started filming. He kept picking me up from my hotel and taking me to different diners. The first time he basically didn't say anything. He would just, like, mumble. The second time he started to run lines with me, which was pretty boring because I already knew the lines. The third time, he ran lines with me again and now I was really bored. The fourth time, he ran lines with me, but then he started going off on these completely different ideas within the scene, talking about crazy things and asking me to follow in terms of improvisation.

So we'd start with the original script and then he'd go off on some tangent and I'd have to follow, and then it was my job to eventually find the space to bring him back to the last three lines of the text we'd already learned.

It was a huge revelation for me, because until that moment I thought being an actor was just acting naturally and saying the lines someone else wrote. Nobody had ever asked me to build a character. The only thing they'd ever done to direct me was to say something like "Say it faster" or "Say it slower." So it was a whole new feeling for me, because I realized acting was not a dumb job. You know, I thought it was a dumb job. Somebody else writes something and then you repeat it. Like, how dumb is that?

There was this moment, in some diner somewhere, when I realized for the first time that it was me who hadn't brought enough to the table. And I felt this excitement where you're all sweaty and you can't eat and you can't sleep.

Changed my life.

>**IF YOU DON'T DO IT** the right way now, it'll never be what it should be—and it's there forever.

>**IT'S ALWAYS** the same old story—the fine line between the money and quality. Do we have to spend this for this? Well, yeah, because if we don't . . .

>**IF THERE'S A SHORTCUT** taken when you're building a hotel, people are going to notice and feel cheated out of something. It's kind of like a movie: Cumulatively, all the shortcuts and cheats take away from the texture.

>**SOMETIMES** if you have financial restraints, it's a benefit. It forces you to come up with a more creative way.

>**I JUST GO** to the theater. Nobody bothers me. I don't even get recognized. I do it a certain way.

>**AS LONG AS** you've got kids, there's gonna be a problem.

>**I DON'T KNOW** if I've been taught anything by my kids. But things are revealed to me. They unfold. Now you're a grandfather. And your kids are giving you advice.

>**IT'S INTERESTING** when your kids give you advice. I had a conversation with my oldest son the other day. He was saying, "You should do this . . . and this . . . and this." Not that I agreed with him on everything. But it was a good feeling.

>**YOU GET OLDER,** you get more cautious.

>**SITUATIONS COME UP** that you've been through and you can see where they're gonna go.

>**GOOD ADVICE** can save you a little aggravation.

>**I JUST HAD** my twins here. They're fifteen. When I was a teenager, there were less restrictions than I put on my kids. But I know those restrictions are important. Yet they have to have room. It's a delicate balance. You say, I survived it. How could they? And yet they do. With a little luck.

>**I MIGHT LAUGH** more now than when I was younger. I'm less judgmental.

>**IT TAKES A LOT** for me to give one of my father's paintings as a gift.

>**I'VE KEPT** my father's studio for the last seventeen years—since he passed away. I've kept it just about the way it was. At one point I was thinking of letting it go. Then I had a gathering of family and friends—you know, to see it for the final time. Videotape it. But I realized it's different in person than it is on video. It's another experience. So I've held on to it.

>**BE BRAVE** but not reckless.

>**NO MATTER WHAT** Marlon did, he was always interesting.

>**SHOWS YOU HOW** primitive things used to be: We had to set up a tripod to videotape Marlon's scenes in the screening room at Paramount so I could study his movements. I played it on a little reel-to-reel.

>**MARLON AND I** never talked about our performances in *The Godfather*. What was he going to say? We knew each other. I spent time on his island with him. But you don't talk about acting. You talk about anything but acting. I guess the admiration is unspoken.

>**YEAH, YOU CAN MAKE** new friends. I recently met a couple of people that are a lot younger than me. It's a nice thing.

>**REALITY IS** this moment.

>**SOME PEOPLE** understand what it is to create something special, and others are thinking what they can get out of it.

>**I'M NOT GOING** to read all the books I want to read.

>**I MIGHT LIKE** to do things that are more *retiring*. Like sit in a place and just look at the view. Take a nice walk. Have a coffee. But not retire. As long as I'm enjoying what I'm doing, why retire?

>**YOU GO THROUGH** a lot of different phases in life. I used to have dessert all the time as a kid. Now I don't eat dessert much. Except when I'm in special restaurants and I tell myself, Well, I'm *here*. I have to have the dessert.

>**NOW IS NOW.** Then is then. And the future will be what the future will be. So enjoy the moment while you're in it. Now is a great time.

BIO   BORN AUGUST 17, 1943, NEW YORK CITY • Interviewed October 26, 2010

>Winner of two Academy Awards for *The Godfather: Part II* and *Raging Bull*
>Accidentally broke Joe Pesci's rib filming a scene in *Raging Bull*
>Co-founded the Tribeca Film Festival to help revive lower Manhattan after September 11

BRUCE DERN

ACTOR, PASADENA, CALIFORNIA • *Interviewed by Cal Fussman*

>**ON THE MORNING** I had to shoot John Wayne, he leaned in to me with a little Jim Beam on his breath—but sober—and said, "Oh, they're going to hate you for this." I said, "Maybe, but in Berkeley I'm a fucking hero." He put his arm around me, turned to a set of ninety people, and said, "That's why this prick is in my movie. Because he understands bad guys are funny. Otherwise, we wouldn't be talking about them 150 years later."

>**I'D EAT BROCCOLI** if it had hollandaise sauce on it.

>**I'VE NEVER BOOED** anybody in my whole life. In the arena, they're doing something I can't do.

>**YOU CAN ARGUE** to me about this guy or that guy, but I've still never seen Ted Williams again.

>**I FORGET NAMES.** I call a lot of people Bud. It works.

>**GET USED TO ONE THING:** Someone will find a way to say no to you every day of your career.

>**MY DEFINITION OF THE WORD** *fearsome* is the house I grew up in. Glencoe, Illinois. It's gone now. It was fearsome because of who came and went. And for me, not knowing as they passed: Do I bow? Do I dare ask them to shake my hand? My grandfather was one of the first non-Mormon governors of Utah, and secretary of war under FDR. On my mother's side of the family, one of my uncles, Archibald MacLeish, was quite a noted poet who won three Pulitzers. There were a lot of important people sitting around the dinner table, and I was little Brucey in white gloves—I pushed my food on my fork to eat, and the white gloves made me stop because they had to be clean. I had to raise my hand to be called upon, and when you raised your hand, you'd better have something interesting to say that captured the table's imagination.

>**IN HIGH SCHOOL** I was a very good runner. I was kind of a star at Penn my freshman year. But we had two or three other guys that were all-Americans. At that level, *gifts* become involved. And the big guy gives gifts to certain folks that he doesn't give to others.

>**WHEN I QUIT COLLEGE,** I was infected with the wonderful malady of going to movies, and I realized that the people on the screen were touching me. Moving me. I said, "Fuck, if I could learn to do that . . ."

>**ONLY TWO SPORTS I WON'T BET:** boxing, because I don't trust it, and horse racing, because horses can't tell me when they don't feel well. The best thing to make money on is World Cup soccer. Three years ago, I had Uruguay to make it to the final four at 100 to 1.

>**I HAD JUST FINISHED** *They Shoot Horses, Don't They?* and gotten married to Andrea. I wrote my mother a letter and asked her for $500. She wrote back saying, *No. The answer is no. You chose the profession that you are in, you were warned how quixotic it would be, and how there was no sign in your growing up that you'd be able to do it. You're not Gary Cooper. You're not Gregory Peck. Come back to Chicago, you and Andrea, live in the house, and I'll put you through Chicago Law School.* From that point on, I was done.

>**IT'S ALWAYS A BASTARD** who teaches tort law.

>**BLACK SUNDAY** is not a bad movie. It's the only film I made that I wouldn't make again. Because you *could* do that—blow up the Super Bowl.

>**INSTEAD OF** fucking shit up, make shit up.

>**EVERYONE WHO COMES TO LOS ANGELES,** whether by Greyhound, airplane, car, train, boat, bicycle, or a hobo on foot, has a chance to get in the room. When you're in that room, you have three fucking minutes. You better leave them with something that will make them lean forward and never forget.

>**GO TO THE EDGE OF THE CLIFF** and do shit that other people won't do. Then find a way to get it done.

>**AFTER THIS ONE PARTICULAR SCENE,** Alexander Payne came over and said, "Was that okay for you? Because I'm not doing it again." Just like Hitchcock.

>**I DIDN'T GO TO MY MOTHER'S FUNERAL.** You can see it in *Nebraska*, in the scene when I go into that old abandoned house where my character grew up and I say, "This is my parents' room. I would have gotten whipped if they caught me in there. I guess there's no one here who's going to whip me now." That's what I mean when I say that movie is as real as I've ever been in a movie. It's about saying the things you have to say to people before they're gone.

>**IF YOU'VE GOT SOMEBODY WHO'S GOING DOWN,** or close to it, get to them and tell them how you feel. Don't bullshit. You don't have to say I hated you or I loved you. You can just say this was how I felt. And thank you.

>**YOU KNOW WHAT** the greatest remedy on Earth today is? Nobody ever prints this, but it's true. It's not a pill. It's not a shot. It's a hug.

>**IF I'M BORING YOU,** ask the next question.

BIO BORN JUNE 4, 1936, CHICAGO • *Interviewed August 23, 2013*

>Received *actual* death threats after his character "Long Hair" killed John Wayne's Will Anderson in the 1972 film, *The Cowboys*
>Father of actor Laura Dern
>Starred in Alexander Payne's 2013 film *Nebraska*, which was nominated for six Oscars and five Golden Globes, including two to Dern for Best Actor

DANNY DEVITO

ACTOR, LOS ANGELES ◆ *Interviewed by Cal Fussman*

>**I DON'T LOOK AHEAD.** I'm right here with you. It's a good way to be.

>**I WALK INTO THIS BEAUTIFUL,** well-appointed office and there's Jim Brooks and a bunch of the others. I had my sleeves rolled up and I throw the script on the table and say, "All right, who wrote this shit?" Nothing happens in the room. There's total silence. And then they just fucking died laughing. I sat in the chair and they couldn't stop laughing. From that moment on, I was Louie on *Taxi*.

>**SUMMERS IN ASBURY PARK** were hot, man, hot. The sand was blistering hot, so you'd run on the beach from blanket edge to blanket edge. When you do, people get mad at you.

>**I ALWAYS WANTED** a swimming pool. The kind where you just go out in the yard and dive in. As a kid, you'd dig a hole, throw in some water, and get a mud pit. That was, like, a big thing in New Jersey. The first thing I did when *Taxi* hit and things starting rolling was look for a place with a swimming pool.

>**MY FATHER** came up through the Depression. He was like a hobo for a long time, on a freight car, traveling through twenty-one states. His whole attitude was, there are three sides to every story, so you gotta make sure everything is copacetic before you commit.

>**I NEVER HAD A PROBLEM** being bullied. I think it's an important thing for kids to know. Have an equalizer with you. The guy who says, "Ain't nobody gonna touch Danny!"

>**WHEN YOU WERE A KID,** you used to hear, "They can allow a certain amount of rat parts in a hot dog." What do you mean you can allow a certain amount? Who says, first of all? And what are you talking about that there's rat parts in my hot dog? Are you kidding me? The Food and Drug Administration allows it? What? Who gave them the permission to allow rat parts in my hot dog? They say, "Well, there's no way to get them out." Well, who put them in in the first place?

>**COMMERCE.** There's a story about Salvador Dalí. Everyone is waiting for him to come to a lecture, and he's late as usual. People are standing out in front of the hall, a fancy Rolls-Royce pulls up, and it's filled with cauliflower. And Dalí is packed in with the cauliflower. That's how he felt.

>**RHEA'S JEWISH.** I'm Catholic. It's always worked well. We do the seders and the Christmas tree. We hide the matzo and have the Easter Bunny. But we don't do things like Lent. We've never fasted when you're supposed to in the Jewish religion. We only do the fun stuff. We took away the burning-in-hell part.

>**IF YOU'RE GOING TO** have kids, there's only one way to go. They have to know they're the most important things in your life, and once you're doing that, there's no way that you could not learn from them, because they just give you stuff constantly.

>**I GUESS** the almighty dollar has totally done in everybody who's got any kind of altruism in their hearts. Nobody's ready to get their balls cut off for what they believe in. Is anybody out there with his dick on the line? Who?

>**ON THE OTHER HAND,** why would you be a politician in Mexico? That's a short lease on life.

>**IT'S NOT A THING** you can put your finger on, because you can never know what Jack Nicholson's thinking. Sometimes we're talking and you just have to go along for the ride because he's always going somewhere.

>**A GOOD PART** for Arnold would be a burlesque lederhosen guy.

>**YEAH,** I've been to the Leaning Tower of Pisa. It's a tower, and it's leaning. You look at it, but nothing happens, so then you look for someplace to get a sandwich.

>**YOU HAVE TO GIVE PEOPLE** permission to laugh. That's why they would always cut to the banana peel in the Laurel and Hardy movies.

>**I COULD INVITE ANYBODY** to this dinner? Anybody? Let's see . . . Enrico Caruso. I'd want to just have a little pasta with him and talk about his life. I'm a big fan of opera. So I'd also like to have Verdi at the table. Paganini would be really interesting because he was tormented by his father. They say that when he played, he was like the devil. I would throw Brando in there because it would make it so interesting. I don't know if he was a raconteur, but wouldn't it be nice to have Elvis Presley over? And, of course, Nicholson. Maria Callas. Leonardo da Vinci. Fellini. It's okay to have a big table, right?

BIO BORN NOVEMBER 17, 1944, NEPTUNE, NEW JERSEY ◆ *Interviewed September 27, 2010*

>Before becoming an actor, worked as a hairdresser
>Originally played the role of Martini in an Off-Broadway production of *One Flew Over the Cuckoo's Nest* and landed his first major role when Milos Forman asked him to reprise it for the 1975 film
>His production company, Jersey Films, made *Erin Brockovich* and *Pulp Fiction*

ROBERT DUVALL

ACTOR, FAUQIER COUNTY, VIRGINIA • *Interviewed by Cal Fussman*

>**SEEING YOUR NAME** on the list for KP or guard duty when you're in the Army is like reading a bad review.

>**WHEN I KNEW NOTHING,** I thought I could do anything.

>**A FRIEND IS** someone who many years ago offered you his last $300 when you broke your pelvis. A friend is Gene Hackman.

>**IF YOU DON'T** have heroes in the beginning, you don't grow.

>**MAKING THE FIRST GODFATHER** was more laughs than making *Godfather II*. That's because Jimmy Caan was in the first *Godfather*.

>**SOMETIMES** I'll be flipping the channels and come across *The Godfather* or *The Godfather II*. I'll say to myself, *Let me watch five minutes*. Coppola made them so beautifully that I end up watching the whole thing.

>**COPPOLA ALWAYS** wanted my mother's crab-cake recipe. He came to my house to talk about doing *Godfather III*, and I wrote it down for him. But I decided not to do *Godfather III*. It boiled down to money. If you're gonna pay Pacino twice what you pay me, fine. But five times? Come on, guys. The thing is, when Coppola left my house, he forgot to take my mother's crab-cake recipe. He kept calling, but I think it was more for the recipe.

>**A YOUNG ACTOR** once asked me, "What do you do between jobs?" I said, Hobbies, hobbies, and more hobbies. It keeps you off dope.

>**SOMETIMES** working fast is better than waiting, waiting, waiting to get it right.

>**"I LOVE** the smell of napalm in the morning. It smells like victory." People come up to me and say it like we're the only two people in the world who know.

>**THE ATTENTION** I get on the street is enough to be flattering but not so much to be a nuisance.

>**ART IS** competitive.

>**WHEN YOU DANCE** tango fast, you have to think slow.

>**I MET MY WIFE** in Argentina. The flower shop was closed, so I went to the bakery. If the flower shop had been open, I never would've met her.

>**I WAS A LITTLE CONCERNED** about being with a much younger woman at first. So I asked Wilford Brimley about it. Wilford is a very sharp guy. He used to be a bodyguard for Howard Hughes. He said, "Let me tell you something, my friend, the worst thing in the world for an old man is an old woman!"

>**YOU NEVER KNOW** how reality is going to coincide with your dreams. You're optimistic, and you go from there.

>**A HORSE IS** not like a dog. It don't love ya.

>**DENIRO,** how's he doing these days? He's got his own set of rules, that guy.

>**WHEN I WAS FOUR YEARS OLD,** I observed a sheepherder eating at my uncle's ranch in Idaho. I couldn't even speak well, but I said to my mother, "That man eats like this." And I started imitating him. All the cowboys and cowhands were laughing at my imitation. So I guess I've always enjoyed characters.

>**I FEEL LIKE** our country is just a big giant kid with tremendous talent—like an athlete. A big giant kid that's made mistakes, but there's a lot of potential.

>**MAYBE I'M WRONG.** But I think if the United States went down, it would be kind of a dark world.

>**SOMETIMES,** when you look back on it, the $10-million-and-under movies are some of your favorites.

>**YOU GET TO** a certain point where your career kind of works for itself—although you can never take that for granted.

>**GETTING TOGETHER** with friends and holding court over a meal is one of the great things in life.

>**SAY HELLO** to Brando and he'd know you wanted to say hello to him, so he'd ignore you. He had a way of playing a game with life. You never knew what to expect. Because other times, out of nowhere, he'd reach out to you in a way that was very special.

>**WHEN I FINISHED** *Lonesome Dove*, I said to myself, *Now I can retire*. I've done something. Let the English play Hamlet. I'll play Augustus McCrae.

>**WHAT IS IT** that Michael Caine says? "You don't retire. The business retires you." So until they wipe the drool away . . .

>**VIRGINIA'S** the last station before heaven.

>**I HAVE** this great horse named Don Manuel—Manu, for short. When your photographer comes, Manu will probably try to get into the picture. He always does, that horse.

BIO BORN JANUARY 5, 1931, SAN DIEGO • *Interviewed October 8, 2010*

>Father was a naval officer; after graduating from college, Duvall served a two-year in Korea with the U.S. Army
>Breakout role: Boo Radley in *To Kill a Mockingbird*; best known for playing Lt. Colonel Bill Kilgore in *Apocalypse Now*
>Won an Oscar in 1983 for Best Actor for *Tender Mercies*

>**I KNEW I WAS TOUCHED** when I was five. I was kind of a goody-goody who could sing like an angel. I would seek hallways and stairwells where the tiles would give a lovely reverberation, and my ears would go, "Fuck me, this is nice."

>**IF YOU DON'T HAVE HUMAN** dignity, you're going to walk in a hunched way. But if you feel yourself pulled at the top of your head toward the heavens, you're a human being with dignity.

>**I MET PAUL** in our school play, *Alice in Wonderland*. He was this funny guy who cracked me up all the time. We moved to junior high school together, started smoking cigarettes. We loved "Earth Angel" and we emulated the Everly Brothers. We would stare at each other's mouths to copy each other's diction. I would watch where the tongue hit the palate when Paul said a *t*. Just where is that *t*? We would be nose to nose. When you're very young, you're insane. You're a fanatic about your loves. The world hasn't shown you how to corral the thing and be normal.

>**WHATEVER YOUR KIDS ARE** comes from you. So whatever irritates, look at yourself.

>**YOU'LL NEVER FIND** the answer to "What's the right hat?"

>**HOW ABOUT ELVIS?** He wasn't quite "the King" when he was younger. As the years went by, he developed a fantastic physical presence. He treated himself like a wonderful jaguar, a platinum cat. That was acquired over the years.

>**A BEAUTIFUL ASS** is a joy forever.

>**NEVER MIND** the transience of show business and popularity. When we hear Ray Charles, we go, "That's a great singer." You don't need a reporter or a writer to tell us. Good is good and it should shine through the years.

>**MANY PEOPLE PORTRAY** the sixties in a caricatured way. They don't get how healthy the sixties were. What a bust-out of spirit in America. How vital! How wonderfully questioning! They don't get that. They just go to the daisies.

>**I FOUND WHEN** my boy turned sixteen, he becomes his own man. It throws the papa a little bit, you know? He has his own haircut, his own sense of clothes. He has his own identity, and it's his. The shift is very challenging. It can happen overnight. One morning they wake up and they have their angle, their slant on who they are. They can hardly figure it out. All they know is "This wasn't me for the first fifteen, sixteen years. But this is me now." You'd better fasten your seat belt, watch, and learn.

>**IT SEEMS TO ME** that at nineteen or twenty, a young man is burning to be great at something. I was. You have a vision that's beyond the neighborhood. You want to make a mark while you're alive. You don't know exactly your future, but you want to be great at it. And *greatness* is an important word. And you dare not tell anybody how extreme and how burning are your visions, because you don't want anybody to mess with them.

>**MONEY, TO ME,** meant if you're watching a movie and you're bored with the movie, you can get up and leave. You don't have to sit through to the end. Money means the absence of things that you have to do when you don't have money.

>**WE MEN NEVER KNOW** what to do about wallets. If it's a bulge in the back pocket, that doesn't do it. Do you go with a money clip?

>**WHAT YOU LOOK FOR** in a woman really shifts over the years. When you're young, the pretty mouth is everything. When you're older, character is everything. Depth. Can you see me when I'm hurting and can you be there?

>**WHEN THE FIRST SONG** goes good, it tumbles into a can-do complex. When you love a little piece of the show, it keeps affecting what comes next. Momentum is everything.

>**YEAH, THERE ARE SOME SONGS** Paul's done where I've thought, I wish I was working with him. I know how to take this way up. There are a few of them. And he'd probably agree.

>**WHEN YOU'RE A KID,** you think adults have more of a balance and solitude. Then you realize they've learned how to posture.

>**WE'RE ALWAYS SAYING** kindness is everything. It's a nice phrase. But have you been kind today? We think we are. But are you sure? Being kind takes work.

>**ONE DAY CAN** really change everything. You wake up in the morning, you're way out of it. You drank too much the night before. You wake up and feel warped as a human being. But one good day of doing things right—eating well, working well, getting a few things accomplished—can leave you in a better place.

>**I'VE CROSSED TWO** continents by foot. I don't know what's next. I used to think, Follow the break of the spring.

>**HOW ABOUT HOW** great life is? The body coordinates itself and fits together chemically and physically. It's just God's gift. It's a goddamn miracle that this gift carries on day after day. The body works! Who can ignore that, who can count on that? Ultimately it breaks down and then you get the truth. Nope, it was only working by the grace of God.

BIO *BORN ARTHUR IRA GARFUNKEL, NOVEMBER 5, 1941, NEW YORK CITY • Interviewed October 26, 2011*

>Has a masters in mathematics from Columbia University
>Split with partner Paul Simon in 1970, the same year that they released the hit *Bridge Over Troubled Water*
>Is passionate about long-distance walking—between 1984 and 1996, he walked across America in 40 increments

RICKY GERVAIS

COMEDIAN, LONDON ♦ *Interviewed by Scott Raab*

>A SORE THROAT means cancer until the doctor says, "Don't be so stupid."

>NO ONE CAN SAY I've failed except me, artistically, because no one knows my ambitions. They don't know what I was trying to do.

>WHENEVER I HEAR someone in TV or a comedian called a "genius," I think, Medicine lost another one. You mustn't put even someone as great as Larry David alongside Newton.

>NEWTON COULDN'T tell a joke. He'd fluff every line, but he had other strings to his bow.

>I'D NEVER TRIED my hardest at anything before *The Office*. I put everything into it and I never compromised—and I learned what an amazing feeling not compromising is.

>WE'VE GOT a little bit of David Brent in all of us. We all sometimes mistake popularity with respect. We all want to be liked. We all wonder whether our perception of ourselves is exactly the same as the rest of the world's. And we all want to feel that we belong.

>THE ONLY THING I ever demanded was final edit.

>STAND-UP is the last bastion of self-censorship outside the novel.

>I NEVER FORGET that I'm still a real person in the real world. I never completely suspend my disbelief in art.

>I LOVE Laurel and Hardy. I love them because they're precarious. I love them because even though outwardly the comedy comes from them saying, "I'm with this idiot, I'd be better off without him," you know they wouldn't. You want them to fucking hug. They found the DNA for comedy, and it hasn't been improved upon.

>THE FUNNIEST PERSON you know isn't a comedian. He's a friend of yours or a family member, because of the absolute wealth of input you have together, the two-way connection.

>AMERICANS ARE TOLD they can be the next president of the United States. In Britain, we're told, "It won't happen to you. Don't be stupid. Don't even try."

>HONESTLY, no one swears like the British. A cockney saying "cunt" is the scariest thing.

>I'M OVERWHELMED with feeling when I see a mountain or a dolphin or when I think of how amazing evolution is. I just know that it wasn't made by design, that's all. And I know that when we die, we're dead. But love isn't an illusion.

>HELL IS GUILT. That's my hell.

>AFTER *THE OFFICE*, the check came through, and it slightly ruined it. Because I didn't want it to be mixed with why I was proud.

>IT'S LIKE A GIANT PANIC ROOM we've got. The whole house—you press a button and steel shutters come down on every window. I have good security. It's fundamental. And we're in the nicest neighborhood in London. You never know.

>I'M NOT PARANOID, though. It's more to do with comfort, privacy, security. Fundamental. You can't enjoy your life if you're worrying about other things.

>I THINK I'm giving the wrong impression—the shutters make me look like a mental case. They just come down over the windows at night, on the inside. When we go to bed.

>I DON'T want to impress people I wouldn't cross the road to talk to. I want there to be a strict door policy at my club. I want to go, "You can't come in. You won't like this. And I don't want you to like it."

>I DON'T LIKE it when people say, "I did it for the money." I don't like it when they go, "I'm just being honest." Okay, fine—but now I can't count you with this other group of people that've never let me down. Neil Young, he's never let me down.

>MUSIC IS STILL to me the greatest art form. I'm in awe of it. A chord can make me feel sick.

>INTELLIGENCE IS certainly linked to violence in hominid evolution, because we were born without armor and claws and teeth. So we had to work out ways to live and to kill, and we were great at it. We're the best at it.

>IF YOU'RE GOING to try serial killing, do it properly. Don't just kill 'em. Kill 'em, fuck 'em, eat 'em. If I was a judge and you came to me and you'd killed twenty people, I'd say, "Did you fuck 'em and eat 'em?" and you said, "No," I'd say, "Get out of my fuckin' courtroom."

>I HAVE A GYM in my house. The thing is, though, I'm only trying to live longer so I can eat more cheese and drink more wine.

>THESE ARE PAJAMAS. They're getting a bit thin, though. I've got to throw these away soon. Nothing bad. They're clean and they're comfortable. Who are we trying to impress?

BIO *BORN JUNE 25, 1961, READING, ENGLAND • Interviewed August 25, 2010*

>Worked in radio before switching to stand-up and then acting
>Created the original *Office* with Stephen Merchant in 2001
>Also the author of the children's book series, *Flanimals*

WHAT (ELSE) THEY'VE LEARNED

SELECT WISDOM FROM OTHER NOTEWORTHY INDIVIDUALS WE'VE SAT DOWN WITH OVER THE LAST FIVE YEARS.

In the end, winning is sleeping better.

— *Jodie Foster, actor*

>**WHEN YOU'RE SICK,** enjoy it. Because there's nothing else you can do.
— *Michael Douglas, actor*

>**THE FIRST TIME I WENT TO THERAPY,** I had to stop going because they were making me hate my parents. — *Chloe Sevigny, actor*

>**WHAT MAKES A GOOD MARRIAGE?** The good fortune of picking the right partner to battle it out with you and never quit on you through the hell storms.
— *Mandy Patinkin, actor*

>**I WAS IN A CONVERSATION** with Nelson Mandela. I talked to him about how he overcame his bitterness and hatred and resentment, and he said, "You know what? People can take a lot from you. They can take everything except your mind and your heart. Those things you have to give away. I decided not to give them away, and neither should you."
— *President Bill Clinton*

YOU HAVE SUCCESS, YOU CAN TALK ALL THE SHIT YOU WANT.
— *Ozzie Guillen, coach*

SILENCE GIVES YOU TIME TO THINK.
— *California Governor Jerry Brown*

>**MOST PEOPLE** aren't good or bad. They're naïve.
— *Jake LaMotta, fighter*

>**THE MORE PANELING IN THE ROOM,** the more trouble you're in. — *Dan Patrick, broadcaster*

>**STAGE FRIGHT** is not a thing about "Am I any good?" It's about "Am I gonna be good tonight?" It's a right-now thing. It helps me. If I went out there thinkin', "Eh, we'll go slaughter 'em," I'm positive something would go seriously wrong. — *Gregg Allman, musician*

>**YOUR CHILDREN ARE SO DOGGONE DIFFERENT.** It doesn't change your principles and the way you raise them, but you have to have your head on a swivel as far as anticipating that they aren't the same and they aren't going to react the same. — *Archie Manning, former athlete, current father of Peyton and Eli*

I think prison might be one of my biggest fears. How can anyone do well in prison? Even to do well, you have to have a really bad life.
— *Michael Cera, actor*

>**REALLY HOT WATER**—so hot you can hardly hold the washcloth—takes the itch away from poison ivy or an insect bite. It's much better than calamine lotion.
— *Michael Eisner, executive*

>**PEOPLE SAY TO ME** all the time, "you have no fear." I tell them, "No, that's not true. I'm scared all the time." You have to have fear in order to have courage. I'm a courageous person because I'm a scared person. — *Ronda Rousey, fighter*

>**LIFE GOES ON** no matter what the hell you do.
— *Leon Panetta, former CIA director*

>**POWER CAN BE LIKE A SWORD,** a very unusual sword. Not only does it have a sharp blade, but a sharp handle. So it cuts into not only the people it's being used against but also into the people who are using it. — *Robert Caro, writer*

IF IT GETS EASY, IT BECOMES LESS INTERESTING.
— *Peter Jackson, director*

>**I MET BILL MURRAY** a couple weeks ago. He's exactly what you think. I was like *Goddamn, I'm just happy you exist. I don't even want anything from you. You make things better just by walking around.*
— *Conor Oberst, musician*

Don't buy a puppy because it's cute.
— Carrie Underwood, singer

>**IT'S PROBABLY HARDER** to admit mistakes when you're 11-17 than when you're 32-4.
— *Mike Krzyzewski, coach*

>**ONE THING I FOUND OUT** for sure in life is, don't hang out with assholes. Surround yourself with good people. Whether they're the best or not, people are capable of learning if they've got good hearts and they're good souls. — *Kid Rock, singer*

>**THERE ARE ALWAYS** absolutely ruthless people who are ready to crush their people for their own self-aggrandizement, but it doesn't mean they are mad. They look to their own interests, they look to their own survival. In that, they are quite rational.
— *Mohamed ElBaradei, diplomat*

A VARIETY OF TEXTURE— THAT'S WHAT MAKES A GOOD SANDWICH.
— *James Spader, actor*

>**THERE'S A POINT** when you have to separate from your father; that's when you become your own man. Later you can come back again. — *Gus Van Sant, director*

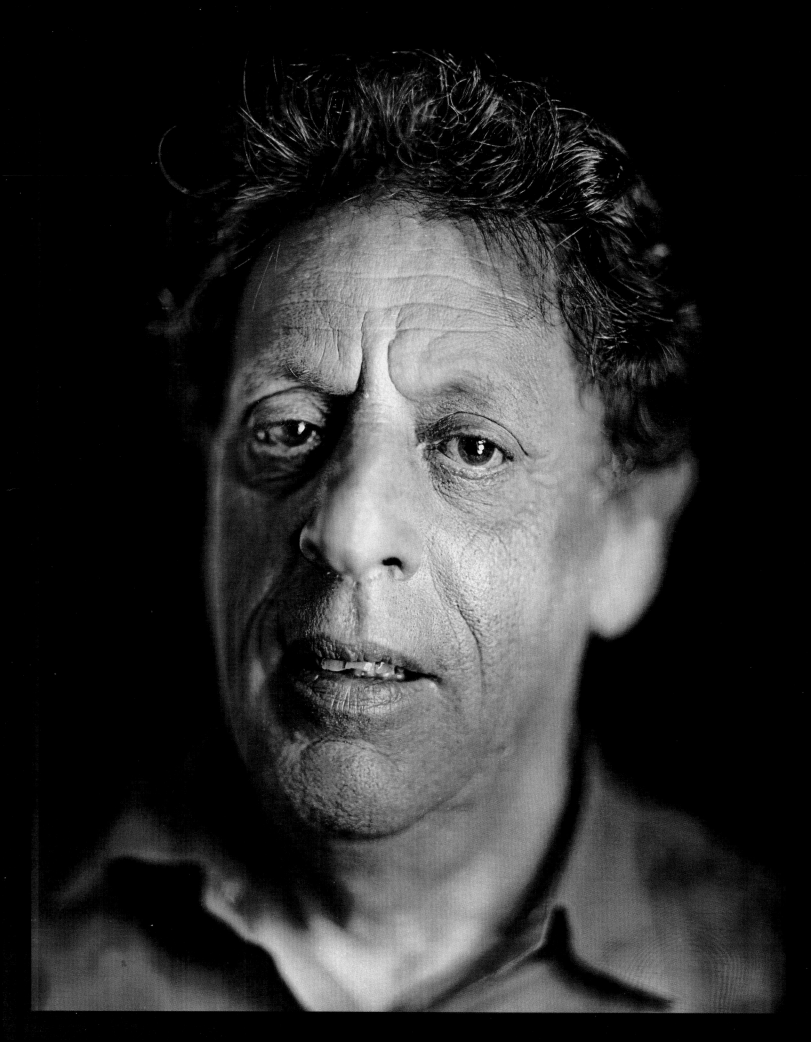

PHILIP GLASS

COMPOSER, MARYLAND • *Interviewed by Mike Sager*

>**I ALWAYS KNEW** what I wanted to do and I did it.

>**A VERY INTERESTING THING** happens as you age. At a certain point you become older than your parents were when they died. My father died at sixty-five. I am now seventy-one. He would have lived longer—it was a mishap, a tragic accident, hit by a car. At this point, I am six years older than my father was when he passed away. I now look at my father as a younger man. It is he who is the young Mr. Glass.

>**WHEN YOU BECOME A PARENT,** you begin to become sympathetic to your own parents. We begin to understand how much we owe to them, how much we're shaped by their vision of the world.

>**I WORK** every morning without fail.

>**I PLAYED MUSIC WHEN I WAS SIX** but I didn't really start practicing until I was eight. What happens is the rewards of work become evident very quickly, especially when you're young. You practice and you get better. It's very simple. And it's a self-reinforcing activity. It's the stick and carrot, really. You apply the stick to yourself and you get the carrot.

>**I WAS NOT** always the brightest bulb in the tree. I was a hardworking guy, but in my opinion I was not one of the most talented people at Juilliard. I didn't have that brilliance that some people really have, but I had a tremendous appetite for the work.

>**MOTIVATION** will make up for a lot of failings.

>**I HAD GONE TO THE UNIVERSITY OF CHICAGO** when I was fifteen, so I was supposed to be very smart, but I never really felt like I was that smart. I just thought that the tests must have been very easy because I passed them.

>**WHEN I LEFT** the University of Chicago, I was nineteen. I went back to Baltimore and announced to my parents I was going to go to music school at Juilliard. They weren't thrilled with that. So I went to Bethlehem Steel and got a job at the steel mill for nine months and made enough money to go to New York and live for a year and work and study music. I didn't think of it as an act of courage; it may have been more of an act of desperation than anything.

>**WHEN I STRUCK** out in my own music language, I took a step out of the world of serious music, according to most of my teachers. But I didn't care. I could row the boat by myself, you know? I didn't need to be on the big liner with everybody else.

>**SELF-ESTEEM** comes from your parents. Somebody tells you that you can do whatever you want, and you believe them.

>**THE QUESTION IS:** What's the mill? Not: What's the grist?

>**DON'T FORGET CULTURE EXTENDS** to every aspect of our life. It covers food and clothes and music and poetry and speech writing and, it covers everything. Everything that you do becomes a cultural dimension of your existence.

>**COLLABORATION IS** the source of inspiration for me.

>**WHEN I WAS A KID** working at the steel mills, when you stood in front of the furnace, the heat that came off was amazing. And I feel that in many ways New York was, for me, the furnace—the cultural furnace. Just standing in that heat warms you up.

>**WHEN YOU HEAR** for the first time the music you have composed, there is that astonishing moment when the idea that you carried in your heart and your mind comes back to you in the hands of a musician. People always ask, "Is it what you thought it would be?" And that's a very interesting question, because once you hear it in the air, so to speak, it's almost impossible to remember what it was you imagined. The reality of the sound eclipses your experience. The solitary dreamer is wondering: Will the horns sound good here? Will this flute sound good there? But then when you actually hear it, you're certainly in a different place. The experience of that is my god.

>**WHEN YOU'RE** really working, really playing tennis, lifting weights, playing basketball, or whatever it is—it happens in sports, it happens in music, it happens in everything—when you're fully consumed with the act, the witness just disappears. And for that reason, when someone asks, "What was it like?" you can't remember, because the person inside of you who does the remembering was otherwise occupied.

>**WHAT I'VE NOTICED** is that people who love what they do, regardless of what that might be, tend to live longer.

BIO BORN JANUARY 31, 1937, BALTIMORE • *Interviewed September 6, 2008*

>One of the most influential composers of the 20th century
>Has been nominated three times for an academy award for Best Original Score and has scored several highly acclaimed films, such as *The Truman Show, Kundun, The Fog of War,* and *The Hours*
>Cousins with *This American Life* host Ira Glass

ELLIOTT GOULD

ACTOR, LOS ANGELES ◆ *Interviewed by Ryan D'Agostino*

>**I HAD NO IDEA** what you would look like.

>**I DON'T KNOW** what's early or what's late in relation to a life.

>**MY FATHER** was drafted—I was in kindergarten. We had pictures of each child in the kindergarten class walking by and saluting my father, who was a private first class.

>**BAY PARKWAY** was a big avenue—*big*. Wide. Although I've been back and it's not as wide as I thought it was.

>**MY PARENTS SAID,** "You won't ever have better friends than us." I thought, If you say so. You're my gods. They weren't right, but they meant well.

>**WHEN MY FATHER** was already gone—he's been gone for nearly twenty years now—his brother told me, "You know, your father never graduated high school." And I thought, *Why are you telling me that?*

>**IT JUST SEEMS LIKE** so many talented people come from Brooklyn. But so many people came here to live. There are talented people everywhere. I mean, we just found out about these 125,000 gorillas who were discovered in the Congo. This is an endangered species. So, I mean, there are undiscovered people in Brooklyn.

>**I DON'T WANT** to be impressed. It distracts me.

>**I SAID TO MICK JAGGER ONCE,** around 1973, "What do you want to do beyond this?" He said, "I'd like to make films." I said, "With your juice, you can." He said, "I know, but I don't have the confidence yet." *Okay?* My seven-year-old son was stuck in the same place Mick Jagger was.

>**THERE IS NO ESCAPE.** There's no place to go. Our life is on Earth.

>**THERE I WAS** in New York, and I had an Islamic cabdriver. At that time I was discovering Hakeem Olajuwon, who was as good as anybody I ever saw. And I said to the driver—I talk to people—I said to him, "As much as I love my children, I know that I don't love my children more than you love your children." We make war with each other because we don't really understand each other.

>**THERE ARE** whole species of fish that can change genders. We have to change.

>**A FREUDIAN PSYCHIATRIST** once asked me if I considered myself to be omnipotent. I said, "I don't know if I know what that word means." He said, "All-powerful." And I said no. But English wasn't his first language—he was from Hungary. I think what he really meant to ask was, *Are you aware that you're oblivious to reality?*

>**IT IS ESSENTIAL** that I listen, so I can try to minimize problems that I create for myself.

>**WHEN BOB COSTAS** asked me if I had ever had a drug problem, I said, No, I didn't have a drug problem. I had a problem with reality.

>**FOR A KID**—or for a repressed, inhibited, shy person—to find out that you could have an effect on people by making a joke was interesting. So I would do that. But I'm not a practical joker. Clooney is. He loves to do that stuff.

>**THE *OCEAN'S* MOVIES** were fun, but it's still business and work.

>**AT AGE TWO,** children are so serious. They're acting like you.

>**MY FIRST WIFE,** Barbra, mentioned the Dalai Lama to me once, and I'm not a wise guy, but I went to Nate 'n Al's delicatessen and I sent her some corned beef, some pastrami, pickles, coleslaw, rye bread, mustard, and I signed it "From the Deli Lama." Now it turns out that he's great. I love him. We haven't met, but he's a great friend.

>**BARBRA AND I** seemed to be so right for each other, as far as ambition and business and identity and power. But it really takes work. My feeling about love is, that part of nature is so precious. I'll always love her. That doesn't mean I want to talk with her.

>**IT'S NOT WOMEN** who are tough. It's life.

>**I LIVE ALONE,** and that simplifies a lot.

>**WHENEVER I DIE,** that will be when I die. What's the big deal? I mean, if I just had some lentil soup, I'd rather not make a mess, but other than that, what's the big deal?

>**WHY?** I know why. How?

>**I HAVE TERM LIFE INSURANCE** until I'm seventy-five. My friend says it's like buying a lottery ticket. Well, I don't want to buy a lottery ticket. I always feel bad afterward, because when I buy it, I think I'm going to win. I don't buy not to win.

>**FRIENDSHIP?** Groucho Marx, in his later days, used to let me shave him. He'd be fully dressed, in his beret, in his bedroom, standing up watching reruns of *Burns and Allen* and *Jack Benny*. And he would let me shave him with his electric razor. What did that mean? That was a form of affection, a form of feeling, a form of confidence and trust.

>**THE BEST FRIEND** I ever had—I don't know that it's a who. "What" would make more sense. Calm is a good friend of mine.

>**I HAVE PERSISTED,** but without a ballpark, without a game, without a team. We go on.

BIO   *BORN AUGUST 29, 1938, NEW YORK CITY* ◆ *Interviewed July 31, 2008*

>Best known for his roles in *The Long Goodbye, American History X, Bob & Carol & Ted & Alice,* and *M*A*S*H*
>Almost drowned while shooting a night ocean scene in *The Long Goodbye*
>Has twice played the voice of God

KELSEY GRAMMER

ACTOR, LOS ANGELES ◆ *Interview by Cal Fussman*

>**PRAYER IS WHEN** you talk to God. Meditation is when you're listening. Playing the piano allows you to do both at the same time.

>**I DON'T THINK DESSERT** is worth it if it's actually good for you.

>**THE GREATEST SIN** is judgment without knowledge.

>**I WANT TO SPEAK** seventeen languages. When you think like that, you'll be consumed by failure. I'm haunted daily by what I don't know.

>**I HAD ONE BAD TEACHER** in elementary school. First grade. All the rest were wonderful. But my first-grade teacher lacked compassion. There was a very specific event: I asked her to be excused several times. That's how we spoke in our family. She asked me, "Number one or number two?" I had no knowledge of what that meant. We didn't talk like that in my family. She proceeded to say that I was being a smart aleck. She said, "If you don't answer me, you're not going." I had no idea. So I urinated on the floor.

>**I DIDN'T HAVE** a divine intervention that said, *This is your calling.* There was one thing I loved a little bit more than surfing—and that was acting.

>**I'VE SURVIVED** the Trojan War. I've been a submarine captain. I've been a psychiatrist. A murderer. I've been a fool. I've tasted all those things. That's a very rich life.

>**THE SIMPLEST** definition of art is a true lie.

>**THE AUDIENCE** is the equal sign in the equation. They tell you what it's worth.

>**IF I EXPECT RESPECT,** I will offer it.

>**I DON'T THINK** there's a universal reason for drug addiction or alcoholism. I do believe in an axiomatic truth: Addiction is the result of unresolved grief.

>**HAVE I BEEN** overpaid? No. Have I been underpaid? No.

>**A GOOD TOMATO** is like a prize.

>**KIDS WILL ASK** the right questions at the right time.

>**PART OF WHAT'S GREAT** about America is that you are not consigned to one existence. You can change your birthright. In fact, one of your obligations is to widen the scope of what your life would have been if you'd been born into it and stayed there.

>**DIFFERENT THINGS** made *Cheers* and *Frasier* special. Both of them, though, were honest. It was the old Shakespeare thing: Hold the mirror up to life.

>**I HAD THE BLESSING** of a heart attack just last year. For me, it was like two elephants standing on my chest. I saw it as a blessing almost immediately. It was almost like the shedding of a skin. It helped me to discard things I didn't need to carry anymore.

>**THERE'S ALMOST NOTHING** better than a baguette and a pound of salami.

>**THE HUMAN EXPERIENCE** reflected in Shakespeare is probably the most specific and uplifting language that we have.

>**"THE FAULT, DEAR BRUTUS,** is not in our stars, but in ourselves, that we are underlings." Okay, I can figure that out. I'm in charge. It was very empowering in a way. You are in charge of your own life. That's a good lesson.

>**I DIDN'T KNOW MY DAD** very well. I spent about three weeks with him when I was twelve, just after my granddad died. That's really all I knew of him. He woke up one night while I was still up and said, "C'mon into the kitchen with me." He pulled everything in the refrigerator out and made some tacos. They were the best tacos I ever had. He was killed about a year and a half later.

>**MY DAD'S DEATH** didn't impact me until I was thirty-eight, which was his age. I got to know my father more in my thirty-eighth year than I ever did before.

>**MY SISTER'S MURDER** was devastating, life changing. I was truly lost by that event, and it took me twenty years to overcome or at least to put in a place where it could no longer hurt me. I'm still saddened by it, but it doesn't hurt me now like it did.

>**NO DAY-TO-DAY** mishaps or indignities can really compromise your sense of self after you've survived a deep tragedy.

>**MY TWO STEPBROTHERS** died in a freak accident. They were snorkeling and were attacked by sharks. One was never found. The other was found washed up on shore. I prefer adversity that I face head-on and can see coming, so at least I get a fair shake.

>**WHAT I CAN CONTROL** is how I react. I can't control anything else.

>**A CHILD IS** a reinvigorating experience. It almost does feel like immortality but not in the way people think. It reminds us there are universal truths that are most simply seen through the mind of a young person.

>**I WAS BROUGHT UP** to never lie. Sure, I have. But in the final mix, the lies I've told are far outweighed by the truths I've lived.

>**IT'S THE WAY OF THE WORLD** that something else will come up that has to be resolved. But I await each day with anticipation and optimism, to quote Auden, to "face with all our courage, what is now to be."

BIO *BORN FEBRUARY 21, 1955, U.S. VIRGIN ISLANDS* ◆ *Interviewed October 21, 2009*

>His character Fraiser was originally only supposed to appear in a few episodes of *Cheers* but ended up staying on primetime television for 20 years, between *Cheers* and *Frasier*
>Won a Golden Globe for his performance as Mayor Tom Kane in *Boss* in 2012, and won two for *Frasier*

ROBERT HASS

POET, SAN FRANCISCO ◆ *Interviewed by Cal Fussman*

>**WHAT'S IT LIKE TO BE NAMED POET LAUREATE?** It means that you spend the rest of your life answering that question.

>**IN A FAMILY WITH ADDICTION PROBLEMS,** people lie to keep things loose. They lie about what day it is, whether your shoes are on your right foot or your left. So early on I learned to avoid unpleasantness . . . in ways that I sort of paid for later in life.

>**ONE DEFINITION OF** *TRUTH* is when someone tells you that the mailbox is on the corner, and you go there, and it's there, then that's true. But the other truth is in that Yeats' phrase, "I feel it in the deep heart's core."

>**YOU KNOW,** Socrates got killed for asking questions like this.

>**THE POET WILLIAM STAFFORD** said he never got writer's block because he just lowered his expectations and kept going. And I heard Wendell Berry say he never noticed anybody get dairyman's block. You get up in the morning and milk the cows.

>**MY YOUNGER BROTHER** once said to my mother, "I don't know why Bob writes poetry. Nobody reads it." And my mother said to him, "Yes, but they don't read it for a long time."

>**WHAT I HAD TO LEARN IN MY SECOND MARRIAGE** was what I needed to unlearn from my family. That is, that things that didn't go well in my first marriage partly because of my avoiding conflict. As you grow, you learn to face up to it.

>**ONE THEORY OF IRISH ELOQUENCE** is that there is no word for "no" in Irish. If you ask an Irishman a question, he'll say, "Well, it's interesting that you ask . . ."

>**YES, THERE'S COMPETITION** when a poet is married to a poet. There's also competition when a poet is not married to a poet.

>**MY WIFE'S IMAGINATION IS SO QUICK** that it makes me feel obvious to myself. Some of it I attribute to the fact that I have good eyesight and she has lousy eyesight. When she was a kid, she was making up the world as it went along. So if we're out hiking, I'll say, "What is that birdsong?" And she'll say, "You mean the one with the orange scribble?" And I'll think, *Damn, I never would've thought of that.*

>**THE PRIMARY MATERIAL OF OUR CONSCIOUSNESS** is the language that flows through our heads. That's the material of poetry. So, starting with the invention of writing, we get a record of what people felt like. Our inner lives are invisible to each other except for what we can read in facial expressions. Starting 2,600 years ago, there's this poem by a young woman on an island off the Turkish coast, saying, "Oh, my god, the way you're looking at that guy while I'm looking at you gives me fever and chills." And suddenly, this first language of what a complicated erotic longing is like is available to us.

>**THIS GENERATION** is comfortable with and interested in poetry in a different way than students were twenty years ago. And I think some of this has to do with hip-hop. Also, instead of talking on the phone, they're texting more. It's a funny version of returning to a nineteenth-century epistolary culture, to have people punching out little messages on a rectangle of aluminum and silicon.

>**I DON'T THINK WE'RE BECOMING MACHINES,** even machines of loving kindness.

>**WE GREW UP IN A COUNTRY WITH APARTHEID.** We saw the Civil Rights movement. You think of the situation of women, the legal rights of women, the possibilities for women, and think about what's happening today. Gay people are supposedly one-sixth or one-twelfth of human beings. They've had to live in some kind of hiddenness and shame. So I say to my students all the time: *I've seen things get better. It can happen. We know it can happen. It's happened before.*

>**IF YOU COME TO SHAKESPEARE'S SONNETS** with a thimble, you take away a thimble full of water. If you come with a bucket, you take more.

>**LAUGHTER** and pleasure seem like the heart of the matter, you know?

BIO *BORN MARCH 1, 1941, SAN FRANCISCO, CALIFORNIA* ◆ *Interviewed November 14, 2014*

>Served as U.S. Poet Laureate from 1995 to 1997
>His book *Time and Materials*, published in 2007, won a National Book Award and a Pulitzer Prize
>Currently teaches at the University of California, Berkley

JIM HARRISON

WRITER, LIVINGSTON, MONTANA • *Interviewed by Cal Fussman*

>**I DON'T SEE** any evidence of wisdom accelerating as you get older. Old people will say it does, but they're generally speaking full of shit.

>**GIVEN FREE REIN,** our imagination can get infinite.

>**A COUPLE OF WEEKS** before she died, my mother—so old and sweet—said, "You've made quite a good living out of your fibs."

>**I'D GONE TO GRANADA** to see where Lorca was murdered on the mountainside by the Franco people. That Franco was a wicked cocksucker, but they certainly never bothered killing poets in America.

>*LEGENDS* **I WROTE IN NINE DAYS.** But that's the only time it ever happened that well. It was like taking dictation . . . but it was after I'd thought about the story for five years.

>**I WON'T EVEN TALK TO YOUNG WRITERS** anymore unless they can give me a good reason. I say, "I don't have any time to talk to you unless you intend to give your entire life over to it, because it can't be done otherwise."

>**ONCE IN TWENTY YEARS** we've had here [in Arizona, where he has a second home] the elegant trogon. It looks sort of like a paint-by-number bird. Very rare bird. You're always so pleased when you have a rarity in your front yard.

>**I PROBABLY WOULDN'T HAVE BEEN A POET** if I hadn't lost my left eye when I was a boy. A neighbor girl shoved a broken bottle in my face during a quarrel. Afterward, I retreated to the natural world and never really came back, you know.

>**IT'S JUST LIKE WHEN I WAS TWENTY** and my father and sister got killed in a car accident. I thought, *If this can happen to people, you might as well do what you want—which is to be a writer. Don't compromise at all, because there's no point in it.*

>**IF ALL I DID** was answer the correspondence I get, that would be my job.

>**IT'S LIKE HUNTING** with Mario Batali. He checked his fancy phone and said, "Fuck. I've got 280 emails." And I said, "What do we do now?" And he said, "Nothing" and put it in his pocket, and we went hunting.

>**I DON'T HUNT MAMMALS.** My friends all do. I love antelope and elk, but I depend on the kindness of friends, because I shot a deer when I was young and it was very unpleasant.

>**UNLIKE A LOT OF WRITERS,** I don't have any craving to be understood.

>**THEY PUBLISHED MY** *FIREFLIES* in *The New Yorker*, and they took a sex scene out of it, which irked me at the time. I said, "That was evidentiary to her character!" She's got to get laid like anybody else at some point.

>**I DON'T KNOW** if it was writer's block or if I just didn't have anything I wanted to say.

>**FIFTY-FOUR YEARS LATER** and we're still married. Very few keepers like that.

>**THE INTERESTING THING** about Nicholson is his inability to lie about anything. It just doesn't occur to him to lie, and that's a rare actor.

>**IT'S OVERWHELMING** when you know Indian history. What fuckin' assholes we were for so long.

>**THE REASON WHY WRITERS** go out to Hollywood is to get some money. Which I still found preferable to teaching. If I can write a screenplay in two months and it pays what I would earn teaching for a year and a half, why not?

>**I REVERE BEARS.** I had a big male bear that I used to leave extra fish about a hundred yards from my cabin. I'd leave the fish on a stump and the bear would eat them. When I would come home from the bar, sometimes he would stop me and I would roll down the window, and he would set his chin right on the doorjamb and I'd scratch his head—but that's stupid.

>**I WORK EVERY MORNING,** all morning, sometimes in the afternoons. Then sometimes I hunt in the afternoons—quail, doves, grouse up north—but just to stay alive, because writers die from their lifestyle but also from their lack of movement.

>**IF YOU'VE WRITTEN ALL DAY,** you don't want to talk about it at the bar.

>**MY GRANDMOTHER LIVED** to be ninety-seven, and I would carry her in and out of the house because she was arthritic and I was real strong then. Grandma said, "This has gone on too long, Jimmy." Ain't that a great thing to say?

>**ALL PEOPLE** disappear.

>**I DIDN'T WANT TO DIE** on the Warner lot.

>**HAS HAPPINESS CHANGED** with age? Yes, I expect less of everything.

>**NO CONCLUSIONS ON TIME.** Other than the old beginning, middle, and end.

>**YOU END UP** missing your dogs.

>**WHAT'S THE MEANING OF IT ALL?** Seems to me nobody's got a clue. Quote Jim Harrison on that: Nobody's got a clue.

>**NOW, WHERE** did I put my cane?

BIO
BORN DECEMBER 11, 1937, GRAYLING, MICHIGAN • Interviewed January 16, 2014

>Writes poetry, essays, novels, and screenplays often concerned with the meaning of manhood and the American wilderness
>His novella *Legends of the Fall*, which was later turned into a film, was first published in *Esquire* in 1979

KEVIN HART

COMEDIAN, LOS ANGELES • *Interviewed by Cal Fussman*

>**AFTER PHILADELPHIA,** the world's easy.

>**I MEAN, YOU GOTTA HAVE SOMETHING.** I couldn't fight. My weapon was jokes.

>**BEING ABLE TO PROVIDE** laughter is a big deal . . . especially in today's time. The one thing that everyone needs is something to laugh at.

>**I THOUGHT I WAS GONNA BE TALL** when I was in the second grade. I was like, *I'm going to the NBA.* But I stopped growing when I was about nine. When I was around 14, it hit me: *I guess this is gonna be it.*

>**I SWAM.** Black guy in the pool. I was a national swimmer. *Pride* was a movie based off an all-black swim team that traveled the world. That's my swim team. We were the real deal. We had guys make it to the Olympic trials. Swimming is a determination sport. You're constantly talking to yourself. *Three more laps. Push it. Push it, One more.* If you think you can't, and you quit in the middle, you're gonna feel like a dick.

>**MY MOMMA SIGNED ME UP FOR SWIMMING.** She signed me up for basketball. She was the one who said: You gotta get your homework done. I am the man I am today because of my mom. She took away my chance of failure.

>**AS A CHILD,** there's nobody cooler than your dad. If there is, something's wrong.

>**YOU HAVE TO PICK UP YOUR VERSION OF WHAT "SMART" IS.** Like, I'm a very intelligent individual. I'm business-savvy. I can break out my company left and right. I understand money and how it comes in and how it should flow out. I understand producing, directing. I understand standup comedy. I understand breaking down the joke. My level of brilliance falls in what I love. But if you give me a book and say, *Kev, read this book, and tell me what you read,* it'll take me three weeks to get through that book because my interest is just not there.

>**TELLING THE TRUTH IS A GREAT GIFT** to have because not many can.

>**I COULD COOK YOU** a peanut butter and jelly sandwich – that's about it.

>**I HAVE A MOGUL MINDSET.** Your opportunities can be as big as your personal expectations for yourself.

>**THE MORE BUSINESSPEOPLE YOU MEET,** the more businesspeople you'll meet.

>**I FINALLY KNOW** how to treat a woman . . . took me 35 years.

>**BABIES ARE UGLY WHEN THEY FIRST COME OUT.** But it was a great moment being there. And now, to see them where they are, having conversations. My daughter does material. "Dad, come hear my five. I got a tight five . . . "

>**A DAY OFF FOR ME ISN'T REALLY A DAY OFF** because I'm with my kids and that's a different type of day off. My kids run me in a hole. But I love it, love it.

>**HOW DO YOU GET THROWN OUT** of a *celebrity* all-star basketball game? You get naked. Start taking your clothes off and throw your shoe at the ref.

>**I WAS IN MY HOUSE THE OTHER DAY.** I just started laughing. I couldn't believe it was my home. Literally, it was an emotional moment. My fans are amazing . . .

>**I HAVE A THEATER IN MY HOUSE.** Doesn't mean I'm gonna stop going to movie theaters. Because if I do that, I'm sheltering my kids.

>**RISK** is going against the grain and then making a U-turn.

>**I SAW CHAPPELLE'S LATEST HOUR.** He's fucking good! So fucking good! I'm thinking: How do I get to be that good? How does that happen? Ball this shit up that you have. Throw it out. You gotta start over. That's what pushes me.

>**IF I DON'T BUST MY ASS** somebody else will.

>**I'M A STANDUP COMEDIAN FIRST.** Nothing's ever going to surpass that. I'm where I am because of standup comedy. That's always going to be number one. Acting is great—but it's a bonus.

>**I THINK THOSE THAT ARE VERY SUCCESSFUL** are those that aren't afraid to tell somebody that they're great.

>**YOU PUT ME ANYWHERE AND I'LL SHINE.** The reason is I appeal to everybody. I don't represent a particular race. I have a multicultural perspective. Wherever they understand English I should be able to do standup comedy.

>**WITHIN THE REALM OF ENTERTAINMENT,** people are always gonna push and push, and those that aren't afraid to will get the rewards.

>**STEAL SLEEP.**

>**THE WORST THING IN THE WORLD** is to say what you assume is the funniest thing ever and hear nothing in response. If you can survive that, if you can stand up from that moment, and shake that moment off, you'll be fine.

 BIO *BORN JULY 3, 1980, PHILADELPHIA, PENNSYLVANIA* • *Interviewed November 18, 2014*

>Worked as a shoe salesman before he became a comedian
>Original stage name was "Lil Kev"
>Once, while performing in Atlantic City, an audience member hit him with a buffalo chicken wing
>Was ejected from the NBA Celebrity All-Star Game in 2012

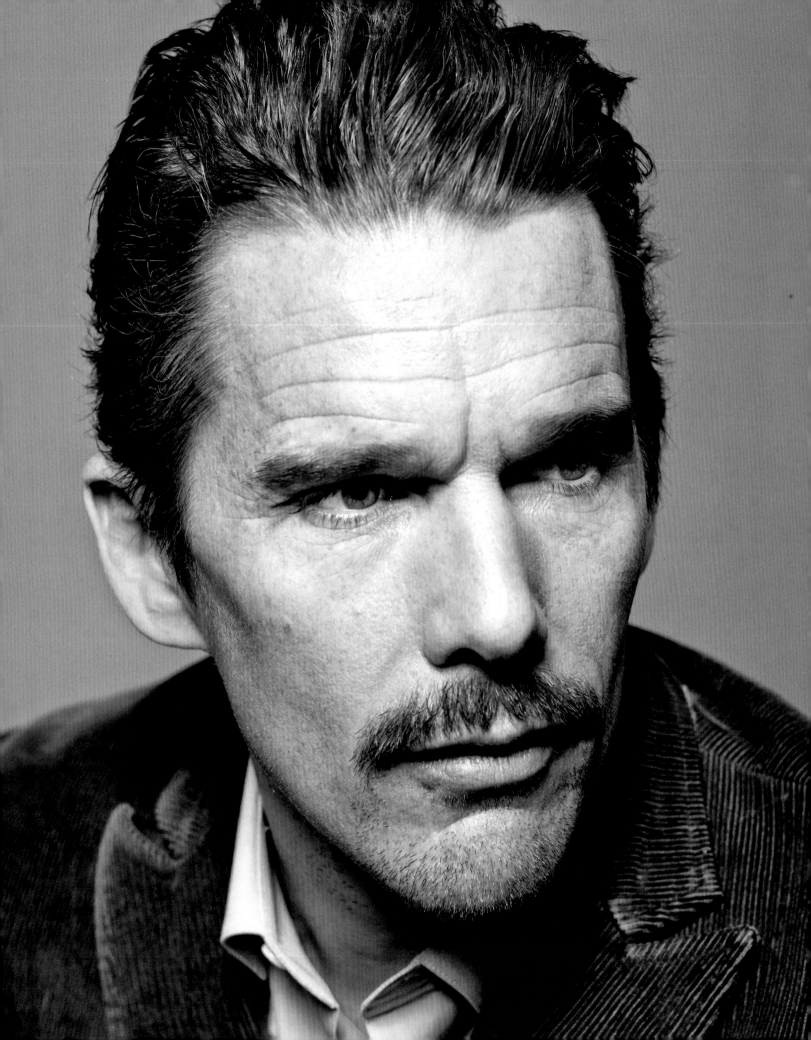

ETHAN HAWKE

ACTOR, NEW YORK CITY • *Interviewed by Mike Sager*

>**WHEN I WAS SIXTEEN,** I remember telling my high school sweetheart I was pretty sure I knew everything. There were some dates of wars and Latin terms I didn't know, but I felt I knew everything that was important. Now I'm forty-two and I'm pretty sure I don't know anything.

>**EVERYTHING ABOUT MY LIFE IS DIFFERENT** than I thought it would be. I don't remember what I thought it would be, but everything about being an adult is so much subtler, and grayer, and so mysterious, and so profound . . . and a lot more irritating than I ever imagined.

>**BEING A PARENT** dilutes your narcissism.

>**THE FATHER HAS A VERY PARTICULAR ROLE,** which involves cutting the umbilical cord, not just as a literal thing but as a metaphor. The father is the guardian of that first step away from the real safety of the nest. Our job is to usher our children into the world.

>**DAUGHTERS ARE EASIER** because I don't project myself into them. Like, if my daughter doesn't like the Yankees, I'm not offended. But if my son says he likes the Orioles, I'm like, "What is wrong with you?"

>**EVERY PERCEIVED FAILURE** turns out to have a secret success, and every perceived success has some secret failing in it.

>**IN *MACBETH*, IT'S FASCINATING TO SEE** the moment when the witches actually come to Macbeth—it's after the biggest triumph of his life. The play opens and he's won two battles and he's the hero of both. Everybody loves him more than ever. *And that's the moment the witches come.* That's what Shakespeare shows: You're not your most vulnerable when you're broke and destitute and hungry. I mean, it's a tough moment, sure. But it's even tougher when the world gives you *everything* you want. That's when you're really in danger of becoming a prick.

>**I LOVE TO TALK ALL THE TIME,** except when I have something to sell. And then I feel like a whore. You're interviewing me because a studio has a giant movie they want to release, and they want the world to go see it. And you're not necessarily interested in me, but you want people to buy your magazine. So the actor is just serving as the tip of the spear. I might as well be standing on the street corner, juggling one of those cardboard arrow signs.

>**I REMEMBER SAYING TO MY SON,** "Who's the best father you ever saw?" And he said, "Dad, you just want me to say you. I don't know any other fathers."

>**ONE OF THE GREAT ADVANTAGES** of not going to college is you're not taught a right and a wrong way to do things. So many young people have stopped freethinking for themselves. I never went to acting school; I learned from Peter Weir, Sidney Lumet, Denzel Washington. I kind of see myself as a perpetual student.

>**WHATEVER YOU'RE DOING,** ultimately we're involved in telling a story and trying to make meaning out of our lives.

>**WHAT WE COMMUNICATE**—our magazines, movies, books, plays, and all that—are our collective consciousness.

>**IN MOVIES,** there's a lot of people working to help you look good. The stage is a much more difficult craft. It asks a lot more of the actor. It's really easy to look like an ass.

>**MY GRANDFATHER WAS** a general manager of the Abilene Blue Sox of Abilene, Texas. He was also the head sportswriter for *The Abilene Reporter-News*. He would cover his own games, which I thought was kind of fascinating.

>**I CAN'T IMAGINE** that there's a person in this world who doesn't have something better to do than tell people that they can't love each other forever, no matter what their sex.

>**WHAT I'VE LEARNED ABOUT DIVORCE?** Not to speak about it publicly. Hopefully that will make somebody laugh.

>**FLIP THROUGH THE CHANNELS** sometime and count how many times you see a woman taking her top off under duress, like being attacked physically, or how many times you see a woman dead, a body or a cadaver. Now flip through and notice how many times we see a man taking his clothes off, a man dead, a man being physically attacked. It's like nine to one.

>**I'M ALWAYS DUBIOUS ABOUT** talking politics; I don't have anything to say about that. To some degree, I think performers should stick to performing, you know what I mean?

>**A LONG TIME AGO, I HAD TO GIVE UP** on the dream of being a professional athlete. Now I have to give up the dream of even playing a professional athlete. But here's the perfect metaphor for aging: I'm starting to look for coach roles.

BIO   *BORN NOVEMBER 6, 1970, AUSTIN* • *Interviewed October 29, 2013*

>Best known for roles in *Dead Poets Society*, *Reality Bites*, *Training Day*, and Richard Linkater's *Boyhood*, a film shot over the course of 12 years
>Has also written two novels

>**SUCCESS NEEDS** no explanation. Failure does not have one that matters.

>**WHEN I GREW UP** in Greenville, every white man was a deputy sheriff.

>**I WAS NEVER** taught to be inferior in my home. I was taught that something was wrong with *them*. It's not that we weren't ready. They were not fair.

>**WE HAD FAITH.** We had hope. But faith is spiritual. Hope is spiritual. At some point, you have to have the law.

>**AFTER WE WON** *Brown* v. *Topeka Board of Education* in 1954, most folks where I lived couldn't understand what that really meant. Civil rights had no meaning to a lot of the older generation. I remember sitting on a porch in Greenville with my grandparents and their friends. Somebody said, "What does integration mean?" I said, "Well, you take salt and pepper, put 'em together, and shake 'em up—that's what it means." Somebody said, "No time *soon*." Oh, that got some laughter. "No time *sooooon*."

>**A MAN WHO** cannot be enticed by money or intimidated by the threat of jail or death has two of the strongest weapons that anyone has to offer.

>**OUR CHARACTER AS A NATION** is determined by how we treat those with the least.

>**JESUS FOUND HIS GRATIFICATION** in restoring the sight of a blind man who had no capacity to help him in return.

>**MY HIGH SCHOOL** football coach taught me to bark signals with authority, or the other ten players will not be inspired. You cannot get a team to move with precision on a weak signal.

>**PEOPLE ARE SCREAMING** for the running back who scored the touchdown. But the lineman knows how he got there.

>**WHAT WAS FUNNY** at one point ain't funny no more. One of my mama's favorite jokes was, "How do you name all them Chinamen? Drop the silverware. Tingtong. Ching-chong." That ain't funny no more.

>**VANITY ASKS THE QUESTION:** Is it popular? Politics asks the question: Will it work? Conscience asks the question: Is it right? The Is it right? question may not be popular. That's why it's the haunting question.

>**EVERYBODY** has a best.

>**OUR GOAL** was not freedom. Freedom was the necessary prerequisite to get to equality.

>**IF YOU THINK** black people have a motivation problem, open up a Wal-Mart and advertise a thousand jobs. Watch five thousand people show up.

>**THIS IS WHAT YOU HEAR:** Kobe made it. The Williams sisters made it. Why don't you work harder? Well, working harder did not solve the problems when the levy collapsed in New Orleans and two hundred thousand people were sent into exile.

>**SOMETIMES IT'S THE CONTEXT.** If Michael Richards is sincere, then you forgive. You redeem, and you move on.

>**WHEN YOU'RE BEHIND,** get up earlier.

>**STORMS COME,** and they are so personal, they seem to know your address and have the key to your house.

>**IF A BLACK DOCTOR** discovers a cure for cancer, ain't no hospital going to lock him out.

>**I SUPPORTED BARACK** in the state senate. I made his case before people knew who he was. There was no plan to attack him. I was talking about a philosophical difference. I had no idea it was being recorded. But locker room trash talk has no place in the domain for responsible leaders. I was sincerely pained by the error and quick to apologize.

>**WE FALL DOWN SOMETIMES.** We fall again and again. Sometimes we're tripped up and sometimes we're knocked down. But however you got down, you don't belong down. Ground is for ground hogs. The ground is no place for a champion. You've got to rise—and function with pain. You must will your way up.

>**WHEN ALL** the dust settles, love covers all.

BIO *BORN OCTOBER 8, 1941, GREENVILLE, SOUTH CAROLINA* • *Interviewed July 24, 2008*

>Joined Martin Luther King's ministry in 1964
>Founded Operation PUSH (People United to Save Humanity) in 1971
>Won South Carolina's Democratic caucuses in 1984 and 1988

SAMUEL L. JACKSON

ACTOR, NEW YORK CITY ◆ *Interviewed by John H. Richardson*

>**I NEVER ASKED** for anything except a purple light saber. George said, "Well, light sabers are either red or green." I said, "Yeah, but I would like a purple one."

>**I WAS RAISED** to be cautious. I went to work with my grandfather, who cleaned office buildings and furnaces, and there would be twenty-year-old guys callin' him Ed, and he called 'em Mister. My grandfather was this old guy, very dignified, but he never looked 'em in the eye. He'd look at me like, "Turn your head down! Don't look the white men in the eye 'cause they'll think you being uppity or arrogant." Now the name of my production company is Uppity.

>**I WAS THE CRACKHEAD** in *Jungle Fever*. I was two weeks out of rehab. I'd been smoking cocaine for a year and a half, two years, and I understood the nature of the disease. I had done the research. So when I started talking to Spike about it, I said, "You don't see him high that much. You always see him when he needs something. He's on a mission to get some shit. That's what I wanna do." And that was my breakthrough. That got me into Hollywood. It was the perfect marriage of experience and opportunity.

>**I DON'T UNDERSTAND** how people live without creating. You know? I don't know how you do one picture a year.

>**WHEN THEY KILLED KENNEDY,** black people were thinking, Oh, my God, white people are gonna come down and kill us all today! All the rights that Kennedy gave us are going away! So they sent us home from school and said, "Stay in the house."

>**I WASN'T ONE** of those people that was gonna walk around and get spit on and get slapped and not fight back. We were doing some kind of crazy things, like stealing people's credit cards and buying guns with 'em. And because of that, some FBI people showed up at my mom's house in Tennessee and told her she needed to get me out of the South or I was either gonna be locked up or killed. So she came to Atlanta and took me to the airport and put me on a plane for L.A.

>**I'VE BEEN SHAPED BY A LOT OF WOMEN.** Honestly. When you come down to it. Between my grandmother, my aunt, my mom, whole bunch of schoolteachers that I had. Then I met my wife, who I've been with for forty-some years. And now my daughter has some part in that. Some hard lessons. Some gentle lessons. I learned to hear what people were saying and not talk while they were talking so I wouldn't miss any of that message. The whole thing was: *Keep your mouth shut and listen.* So I learned to listen.

>**WHEN I CAME TO NEW YORK,** it was bubbling. We watched each other, we encouraged each other, we went to auditions together, we rode trains together, and every Monday we had great parties. But it was also a time of, you know, drugs.

>**ALL OF A SUDDEN,** Morgan's gone. *Boom*. Then Denzel's gone. The opportunities were there, but I was just never prepared because I was a little bit off, you know? And then when I finally got it together—*boom*! It just happened.

>**I ALWAYS WANTED** to do a big pirate picture.

>**I HAVEN'T HAD** a drug dream in ten or twelve years. All of a sudden, I had one, like, two weeks ago. Even in the dream, you're hiding shit from people! People that you know pop up in the dream and you got this big-ass ball of cocaine in your hand and you stick it behind your back and go, "Yeah, I'm all right." And then you wake up and you feel as bad as if you'd actually done it.

>**I WENT TO THE MOVIES** a lot when I was a kid. That was my joy. Saturday mornings, my mom kicked me out of the house, I went to the movies at nine in the morning and watched cartoons and serials and the double-feature horror picture, and then I would meet her later for the adult stuff. So I love movies that way. So I'll do a movie like *Snakes on a Plane*, and I'll do a film that's very serious. And I'll do a comedy, because it's there.

>**I'VE NEVER BEEN TO JAIL.** I've never been arrested. I've never been locked up. I'm a good son, a good father, a good husband—I've been married to the same woman for thirty years. I'm a good friend. I finished college, I have my education, I believe in education, I donate money anonymously. So when people criticize the kind of characters that I play onscreen, I go, "You know, that's part of a story."

>**I WANNA BE** a scratch golfer for at least one month in my golf career. That's all I want.

>**MY DAD WAS** an absentee dad, so it was always important to me that I was part of my daughter's life, and she deserved two parents, which is part of what informs us staying married for thirty years. 'Cause everybody has a chance to say, "Fuck it," and walk away, you know? But you also have a chance to say, "Okay, fuck it, I'm sorry." Even if you're not.

BIO BORN DECEMBER 21, 1948, WASHINGTON D.C. ◆ *Interviewed October 1, 2010*

>The highest grossing actor of all time, according to the *Guinness Book of World Records*
>Had a stutter as a kid
>Served as an usher at Martin Luther King Jr.'s funeral

JOAN JETT

MUSICIAN, NEW YORK CITY ◆ *Interviewed by A.J. Jacobs*

>**THERE'S THIS THING** that happens when a guitar chord is struck a certain way—it slightly bends out of tune and then goes back into tune. And there's a connection from that sound right through your crotch, right up into your heart.

>**THEY'VE TURNED** the word *rock* into nothing. It's a meaningless word. "It rocks." "That food rocks." "She's rocking in that outfit." They've taken the word and stripped it of all its menace, of all its dirt, of all its sex.

>**POP MUSIC** is not a threatening style of music. It's music that says, Take me for what you will. Rock 'n' roll says, You're mine, motherfucker.

>**WHEN PEOPLE** said to me, "Girls can't play rock 'n' roll," I'm like, What are you saying? Girls can't master the instrument? I'm in class with girls playing cello, violin, piano, Beethoven, Bach. You're telling me they can't play guitar?

>**I LEARNED** to scream from Marc Bolan of T. Rex.

>**NOBODY KNOWS** what anticipation is anymore. Everything is so immediate. No more standing outside Tower Records in a long line.

>**I REMEMBER TIMES** when I was at shows and the person onstage locked eyes with me. And in that moment, everything was right with the world. I think that's part of my job, to create these thousands of moments every night. And for the rest of their life, they can say, "You guys looked at me," or "You sweated on me," or "I got your gum."

>**I LIKE THE WAY** black looks. I think I look better in darker clothes. And maybe the fact that I wear black so much makes me more aware of putting people at ease. The black is sort of the bad-guy guise, so I work overtime to make people comfortable.

>**THE SUN,** the smoking and drinking—I avoid them. I have friends the same age as me who do those things, and it's a whole different deal.

>**DON'T BE AFRAID.** Because you're going to be afraid. But remember when you become afraid, just don't be afraid.

>**THEY SAID,** "Lose the guitar. Maybe you'll be more palatable without the guitar."

>**PARTLY, I LIKE** a bad reputation. But I also want a reputation of being a good person.

>**I THINK SOME** of our lyrics that might be considered angry, if they were sung by a guy, they'd be called passionate or intense.

>**I DON'T LOOK** good in beige.

>**WHEN YOU'RE ONSTAGE,** you just have to empty out and stay as empty as you can and let it come in. It's like you're driving around in your car and all of a sudden, you wind up on the other side of town, and you're like, How'd I get here?

>**THE NATIONAL ANTHEM** is a very hard song to sing. You gotta start in the right spot or you're screwed.

>**I NEVER LIVED** in Wisconsin. One of those images you see as a kid—I might have been six or seven—it was a *Sports Illustrated* cover. Everybody was completely muddy, so muddy you couldn't see who was wearing what uniform. One guy had a swipe across the helmet where the mud was wiped off, and you could see part of the G through it. For some reason, as a kid, just seeing that G, I became a Green Bay Packers fan. Isn't that weird?

>**IF YOU'RE A WOMAN** who doesn't wear a dress, you are gonna take shit. If you're a woman who doesn't wear a dress and shaves her head, forget about it.

>**WHEN I WATCH** these cop shows, I think of how many things boil down to: Someone's pride was offended. Somebody was disrespected.

>**WHEN THE RUNAWAYS** broke up, I didn't know what I wanted to do. A breakup is like losing a very good friend. It's like a death.

>**I WAS MIKE TYSON'S** wake-up call for several fights—he would have me call him on the morning of a fight. He was so sweet to me.

>**I WAS ONSTAGE** when Howard Dean did his famous yell. It was completely blown out of proportion. The press couldn't even get the emotion right. They were saying he was angry. No, he was *effervescent*.

>**I DON'T THINK** about the shouting. Should I do it high, do I do it hard? I just do it. It's guttural.

>**IN THE BEGINNING,** I used to eat discarded food off other people's Holiday Inn trays. I mean, it was discarded.

>**PEOPLE COME UP** and stab you, give you a shot in the ribs with one finger, like you're the Pillsbury Doughboy. They want to see if you're real. They have a sense of ownership. You're public domain, to be touched, like with the Statue of Liberty.

>**I DON'T GOOGLE** myself. Never read message boards, either, because that's even more dangerous.

>**BEING IN A BAND** is like being in a family. It's intense, it's emotional. It's not always smooth. In fact, something's kind of weird if it *is* smooth.

BIO *BORN SEPTEMBER 22, 1958, WYNNEWOOD, PENNSYLVANIA* ◆ *Appeared in the November 2011 issue*

>Had a number 1 hit with "I Love Rock 'n' Roll" in 1982, with her band The Blackhearts
>Other hits include "Crimson & Clover" and "Bad Reputation," which served as the theme for the show *Freaks and Geeks*
>First band The Runaways inspired the film of the same name, starring Kristen Stewart and Dakota Fanning

QUINCY JONES

MUSICIAN, LOS ANGELES ◆ *Interviewed by Cal Fussman*

>**OKAY,** let's have some fun.

>*HELL NO*, **IT HASN'T ALWAYS BEEN FUN.** I started at the bottom. Growing up in Chicago, biggest ghetto in America during the Depression. Mother went insane. That's not fun. But you know what, you have to find your own joy, don't you?

>**WHEN YOU ASK GUYS LIKE SINATRA AND RAY CHARLES** to jump without a net, you better know what you're talking about.

>**YOU NEED THE GIFT** to write a song. Everything else you can train for. But the melody comes straight from God.

>**CHERISH YOUR MISTAKES** and you won't keep making them over and over again.

>**IT'S THE SAME WITH HEARTBREAKS** and girls and everything else. Cherish them, and they'll put some wealth in you.

>**WHEN I WAS YOUNG,** Ben Webster told me, if you get the chance to go overseas, eat the food the people eat, listen to the music they listen to, and learn 30 or 40 words in every language.

>**I'M STUDYING MANDARIN NOW,** and Arabic. Open the door to them, and they'll open it to you.

>**I WAS ELEVEN WHEN I KNEW.** I was living in Bremerton, Washington, near the shipyards where my father worked during World War II. Some kids and I heard there was some pie coming into the rec center that we called the Armory. We found the freezer where they stored ice cream and stuffed ourselves with lemon meringue pie. Then I broke open the room next door. There was a spinet piano in there. I almost closed the door. But something told me to go back in there. I touched that piano, tinkled the keys, and knew in every cell of my body that music would be my life for the rest of my life.

>**"NOT ONE DROP OF MY SELF-WORTH** depends on your acceptance of me." That's the way Ray Charles and I lived every day. We had to make up our own rules.

>**A GOOD MARRIAGE?** Attention. Giving each other space. Protecting each other's privacy. It's hard. 24-7 is a long time. I've never been bored or lonely in my life. I like to read, I like to write. Listen, dream. So I would say that four days a week is enough for me. I need three off for me.

>**WHEN YOU CHASE MUSIC FOR MONEY,** God walks out of the room.

>**BONO IS LIKE MY BROTHER.** We had a twenty-five-minute meeting with the Pope for third-world debt relief.

>**NOT LONG AFTER,** the paper said because of that trip we got twenty-seven and one-half billion dollars in debt relief for Mozambique, Bolivia and the Ivory Coast. Two raggedy ass musicians, Irish rockin-roller and a brother from Chicago. We were haaaaaaaapy. Like a fox eating sauerkraut.

>**GORBACHEV WAS A HERO.** A great man. And Russia and America shit on him.

>**THE RELATIONSHIP BETWEEN A PRODUCER AND AN ARTIST** is heavy. His whole future is in your hands. The artist is crazy if he's got a producer in there he doesn't trust.

>**THEY DOUBTED ME ON MICHAEL FOR** *THRILLER*. I found the power in being underestimated. It's the greatest place to be.

>**WHAT'S SPECIAL ABOUT MARLON BRANDO?** Everything is special about Marlon Brando. Marlon was a piece of work, man. Marlon was nanotechnology. Nanotechnology that's one billion times faster than the computers we have now. That's Marlon.

>**SINATRA DIDN'T HAVE ANY GRAY.** He either loved you or rolled over you with a truck in reverse.

>**BEFORE EVERY BLACK ACTIVIST MOVEMENT,** there's always been revolutionary music. It was bebop that came just before Martin Luther King and Malcolm X.

>**MUSIC IS MATHEMATICS.** I didn't want to hear it at first because it sounded technical. But it's true. And it's one of the few things in the world that engages the left brain and the right brain, your emotion and your intellect, simultaneously. Romance does that, too.

>**THEY THOUGHT I WAS GONNA DIE AFTER THE FIRST ANEURISM.** They had a tribute for me. Marvin Gaye. Richard Pryor. Cannonball Adderly. Sidney Portier. It was scary – like looking at your own funeral. Good news is, you've lived. Bad news is, you've got another operation coming in two months. The trouble was the doctors said, "You can't get excited." How the fuck am I not going to get excited looking at all the people I love out there doing a show?

>**I'M PROUD** of everything I ever made, man.

>**YOU WANNA SEE MY HEART?** Look at my daughters.

BIO ◆ BORN MARCH 14, 1933, CHICAGO, ILLINOIS ◆ *Interviewed July 30, 2008*

>First instrument he played was a stride piano in his neighbor's apartment (he was five)
>Co-produced Michael Jackson's *Off The Wall*, *Thriller*, and *Bad*; has worked with Ray Charles, Frank Sinatra, Aretha Franklin, and dozens of others
>Nominated for a record 79 Grammys; has won 27
>Is a devotee of Hatha Yoga

LARRY KING

TALK-SHOW HOST, LOS ANGELES • *Interviewed by Cal Fussman*

>**EVERY OPHTHALMOLOGIST** I've known wears glasses.

>**SOMEONE TOLD ME** there was a front-page screamer on top of a newspaper in New Zealand: LARRY KING LEAVING SHOW. Who knew I was that big in Auckland?

>**YOU CAN'T HAVE HAPPINESS** without having had unhappiness, because how else would you know what's happy?

>**I NEVER LEARNED** anything while I was talking.

>**THE SECRET** to my success is brevity. Sincerity. And, above all, curiosity.

>**YOU NEVER SOUND** like you to you. I don't hear my voice as raspy as you do. When I hear people imitate me—"Altoona, hello!"—that ain't me, to me.

>**QUESTIONS ABOUT** my marriages and divorces always take me to the same place. I once asked Stephen Hawking, the smartest guy in the world, what he didn't understand. He said, "Women." If the smartest guy in the world couldn't understand them, what do you expect from me?

>**GREAT ATHLETES** never have lousy names. If your name is Frederico Trepalano, you are not going to be a great ballplayer.

>**MICHAEL JORDAN** is a great name. Easy to remember. Seven letters and six letters. Usually, if they combine to thirteen, they're good names. I'm into numbers.

>**THE THREE GREATEST WORDS** in the English language are not: *I love you*. That's second. The first are: *Leave me alone*.

>**I'M AGAINST** capital punishment in all cases except meter maids.

>**LOOK AT THAT:** five new voice mails. Never heard the phone ring once. If I could fix something, I would perfect cell phones.

>**WHAT MAKES** one jockey better than another? Horses run for him.

>**THERE'S A DIFFERENCE** between funny and mean.

>**YOU CAN'T DO** anything about anything you can't do anything about.

>**GEORGE BUSH FORTY-THREE** was the only president I ever met who was exactly on time.

>**BILLIONAIRES** never say they're billionaires.

>**PEOPLE WITH MONEY** say money isn't important. I never heard a poor person say money isn't important.

>**SINATRA** was so sad at the end of his life. He told me, "All my friends are gone."

>**IF YOU HAVE** two friends in your life, you've got a bounty.

>**HOCKEY I CAN TEACH** you in a day. Basketball is basically an understandable game. But it's impossible to teach baseball to an adult—too many nuances.

>**FLYING PRIVATE** is the world's greatest luxury. You don't get jet-lagged.

>**IF YOU'RE FROZEN,** you die with a modicum of hope. No other people have hope, except those who believe.

>**BELIEVERS** are in a no-lose situation. They're either gonna be in a better place and then they'll know it. Or they won't be in a better place— but they'll never know it.

>**I CAN'T REMEMBER** the last time I bought a pair of suspenders. A lot of people send them to me. Ryan Seacrest sends me all my jeans. I have eighty shirts in the closet. You want a shirt? What do I need eighty shirts?

>**I HAVEN'T HEARD** Rush Limbaugh in ten years. The last time I heard him, he told an absurd lie. I could never listen again.

>**I STILL REMEMBER** drinking out of a water fountain that said colored when I arrived in Miami in 1957. The biggest change in my lifetime has been civil rights.

>**I HAVE TWO YOUNG BOYS.** Ten and eleven. Three grown. A stepson. A house. When did it all happen? I'm still the nine-year-old kid walking into Ebbets Field.

>**TO NOT USE** technology to help officiate sporting events is insane. It's: Okay, we'll accept bad.

>**WHEN YOU GET MY AGE,** you shouldn't have to do what you don't want to do.

>**THE** toughest part was saying good-bye to the staff. They were losing their jobs and they were crying for me.

>**RETIRE?** To what? I'm not retiring. I'm just leaving the show. I could never retire.

>**PEOPLE ARE TELLING ME** that Larry King is a brand. I always thought Pepsi-Cola was a brand. But people are trying to figure out how exactly to brand me. So if they get a good soldering iron . . .

>**BILL MAHER** couldn't believe how funny I am. The public don't know the funny part of me. They're gonna find out.

>**IN THE WORDS** of Louis Armstrong, "I see trees of green, red roses, too . . ."

BIO *BORN LAWRENCE HARVEY ZEIGER, NOVEMBER 19, 1933, NEW YORK CITY* • *Interviewed July 1, 2010*

>Hosted *Larry King Live* from 1985 to 2010, and *Larry King Now* since 2012
>Married eight times
>Loves suspenders

PADMA LAKSHMI

HOST, MUSE, AUTHOR, NEW YORK CITY • *Interviewed by Cal Fussman*

>**WHAT IS IT** that you do where you lose track of time? That's what you should spend the most time doing.

>**THE BEST THING** you can do for someone is make them a beautiful plate of food. How else can you invade someone's body without actually touching them?

>**CANADIAN BACON** is best left to the Canadians.

>**I LIKE** the crispy, curly, crunchy, maple-coated, caramelized, blackened slowly kind of bacon on the back of a greasy grill at a five dollar diner at 4:00 a.m.

>**BEAUTY IS** something that commands your eye to look at it.

>**DO I LIKE TO WRITE?** I like to have written.

>**A GOOD PIECE** of writing is as joyful as the face of a beautiful woman. But it's a lonely exercise.

>**HAVING A SWING** hanging in your living room puts you in a good mood.

>**SEX IS AN ACT.** Love is a way of being. Both are very enjoyable to engage in. Both can be in short supply sometimes.

>**IT DOESN'T MATTER** how precisely the onion is cut as long as the person chewing it is happy.

>**THERE'S ONE THING** about being pregnant: I missed boxing. Boxing is as much about absorbing and sustaining pain as it is about inflicting it. It is also about stamina. The exercise and the physical meditation taught me a lot.

>**YOU CAN'T SPAR** and say, "Not the face."

>**I'M NOT OF THE AMERICAN ILK** that, you know, your lover needs to be your best friend and know you inside out. I think he should know you well enough to please you. Otherwise, what secret will there be to tell him when you're ninety?

>**I'M NOT SUPPOSED** to say this, but my ex-husband was very impressive. That's how I fell in love with him.

>**THE PARTING?** I think you always learn a lot when you leave an important stage in your life. With every kind of growth, there's a lot of pain.

>**I LIKE WATERMELON** with salt.

>**EVEN AT THIRTY-NINE,** I look in the mirror and see the same girl getting ready for sophomore class in high school, wanting to look nice, wanting to be accepted and appreciated and admired. I don't think you stop that. I don't want to stop it, because I want to have all the hope of a fifteen year old, too.

>**A FRIEND IS** someone who's always there at the right time and not there at the right time.

>**ALL CHEFS ARE** like Jewish mothers. They want to feed you and feed you and impress you. It's an eagerness to please.

>**IF YOU WERE GOING TO BE** a judge on *Top Chef*, my advice would be to think like a customer and not like a chef. Don't say, "I would've done this." Because it's too late—and you're not doing it.

>**I NEVER WORKED** as a model in Japan. Girls went to Japan and they came back with suitcases full of money. But I never got invited because I know what they like. They like blond girls, they like flat-chested girls, and they don't like dark girls. On the other hand, I could mint money in Italy in the nineties. Both had to do with local preferences.

>**IF A WOMAN IS DRESSED UP** like a million, her hair is done, she's got the perfect shiny shoes, and the bag, and the this and the that, and she smells exactly as she should, it's just too much artifice. Food is the same way.

>**I USE CORNFLAKES** in my fried-chicken recipe. I use toothpaste to polish my silver jewelry. I use honey to exfoliate and cleanse my skin. The most natural, simple, nontechnological approaches to chores and events are the routes I find most attractive.

>**SPICES SHOULD** draw the eye to what they're spicing up.

>**WHEN I MAKE JEWELRY,** it's so that a woman is adorned. When a woman walks into a room, you should notice her. You should notice her smile, you should notice her eyes, you should notice the nape of her neck or the curve of her back. You shouldn't notice the loud dress or the big earring. Stones and metals are the equivalent of spices.

>**I'LL BET** if you ask your wife if she's going to have her period on the weekend of March 15, she would be able to tell you.

>**MY GRANDPARENTS** had an arranged marriage. I don't think I ever heard them once say "I love you" to each other. And I don't think I ever had greater evidence of it.

>**MY DEFINITION OF COURAGE** is someone who tells the truth all the time. I'm a big believer in telling the truth and going forward even when you know that it's going to bring a lot of strife into your life.

>**RITUALS OF DEATH** are for the living. The dead have had their experience with it, and it goes with them.

>**EVERYTHING TASTES BETTER** when you eat it with someone you love.

BIO *BORN PADMA PARVATI LAKSHMI VAIDYNATHAN, SEPTEMBER I, 1970, CHENNAI, INDIA • Interviewed February 8, 2010*

>Has worked as a model, actress, author and TV host, cohosting *Top Chef* since 2006
>Married to novelist Salman Rushdie from 2004 to 2007

JERRY LEE LEWIS

MUSICIAN, NESBIT, MISSISSIPPI ◆ *Interviewed by Scott Raab*

>**I GOT GOOD HEALTH,** I still got pretty hair, I'm still rocking. That's sitting on top of the world about as high as you're going to get.

>**I DON'T HAVE** a lot of talking to do, because I've got a show tonight. Oh, about three minutes. But putting the makeup on and getting ready and going out there, setting down, and going to the piano, and leading you out there, and setting down—by the time you do "Great Balls of Fire," which is a minute and forty seconds, you've done killed two hours. You might as well have done a whole show.

>**I WORK TO PLEASE** my audience. I was watching those people last night. I was watching their eyes. And I got into it a little. They was getting into it. That's very important.

>**I NEVER SET** fire to a piano. I'd like to have got away with it, though. I pushed a couple of them in the river. They wasn't any good.

>**A BIG GRAND**—I just pushed it down a hill. If it hadn't been downhill, I'd have never made it. Conway Twitty and them's eyes got that big around.

>**I'VE ALWAYS** showed up. If I got paid.

>**I'D RATHER NOT** get into that.

>**I'D RATHER NOT** get into that, either.

>**I KNOW** you're not trying to be rude.

>**I'VE LEARNED** to be one of the hardheadedest cats in the world. I've learned that. Yeah. My daddy told my mama—I wanted to go get married the first time, and boy, she was crying and carrying on, and my daddy said, "Leave him alone, Mammy. You know how hardheaded he is. Hardheaded as a rock." I was sixteen. That was in Louisiana.

>**I NEVER WAS MUCH** on picking cotton. I just didn't see no future in picking cotton. Or chopping cotton. I says, "You know, Daddy? This is ridiculous. I'm a piano player." And he says, "Boy, pick your cotton."

>**WENT TO BIBLE SCHOOL** in Waxahachie, Texas—Southwestern—for about fifteen minutes. It was fire and brimstone. This boy was a young preacher, and he wanted to sing "My God Is Real," and he said, "Would you play the piano behind me?" I said, "Sure, I'll back you up. How you want to do it?" And he started singing. I said, "Nope, nope—that's not going to get it. You want to do it like this," and I give him a good solid beat. And he sung it, and we both got expelled.

>**I WAS DUMPING** that cement out of that wheelbarrow—Mr. Chalmers Durant hired me—and I was out there with those big guys—I mean, giants—and I says, "Mr. Durant, you think you can put me on that sand pile over there?" He said, "Well, son, if you hadn't been a bull, you shouldn't have bellowed."

>**I SOLD SEWING MACHINES** for Atlas—Atlas Sewing Machines, centered out of Baton Rouge, Louisiana. That didn't last too long. That's when I was going back and forth to Memphis to get my record out.

>**THERE'LL NEVER BE** another Sam Phillips and there'll never be another Jud Phillips—two characters that made music what it was.

>**IT'S JUST SOMETHING** that comes to you. One day you're fifteen years old, and music's coming to you. You're playing.

>**I WRITE.** I got songs.

>**I'M ASHAMED** to say that I haven't been to church in quite a while, but I intend to get myself back into going to church again. I'm not going to lie about it—I just haven't kept up with it like I should.

>**I NEVER THOUGHT** about writing a book. Everybody else has written one. But one day I'll write the real truth down—the real truth. Then I'll go to the penitentiary.

>**I NEVER WENT** to the penitentiary. Close, but I never made it in.

>**IF I COULDN'T** do it my way, I'd best stay at home.

>**WE DIDN'T DO** too much talking. Mostly action. But that's been a long time ago. I've learned to mellow. I'm not as wild as I used to be.

>**I DON'T DRINK** anymore. I can't handle it. It breaks my face out, my skin. I didn't think anything could ever make me stop drinking, but there's always something that can make you stop drinking. God can make you stop drinking. He can cut your water off.

>**I'M FOOTLOOSE** and fancy-free. I had a couple of pretty good wives. I blew it. Together, we both blew it. It just didn't work out.

>**I GOT MY GUNS** at home. I got a .347 Magnum, got another pistol. That brown one, it's like a brand-new looking pistol. It's in a holster. It's one that Kerrie give me—that's a wife gone by. If I had it all to do over, I'd do the same thing again. I think I would, because if I didn't, I'd miss out on something great. I've had some great times. I wouldn't want to miss out on great.

>**I ONLY WORK** for people that I know have the money and they're going to pay you. I ain't done too bad.

BIO

BORN SEPTEMBER 29, 1935, FERRIDAY, LOUISIANA ◆ *Appeared in the January 2013 issue*

>Achieved global stardom with "Whole Lotta Shaking Goin' On" and "Great Balls of Fire" in 1957; later went on to become a country music superstar
>Inducted into the Rock and Roll Hall of Fame in 1986
>Married seven times

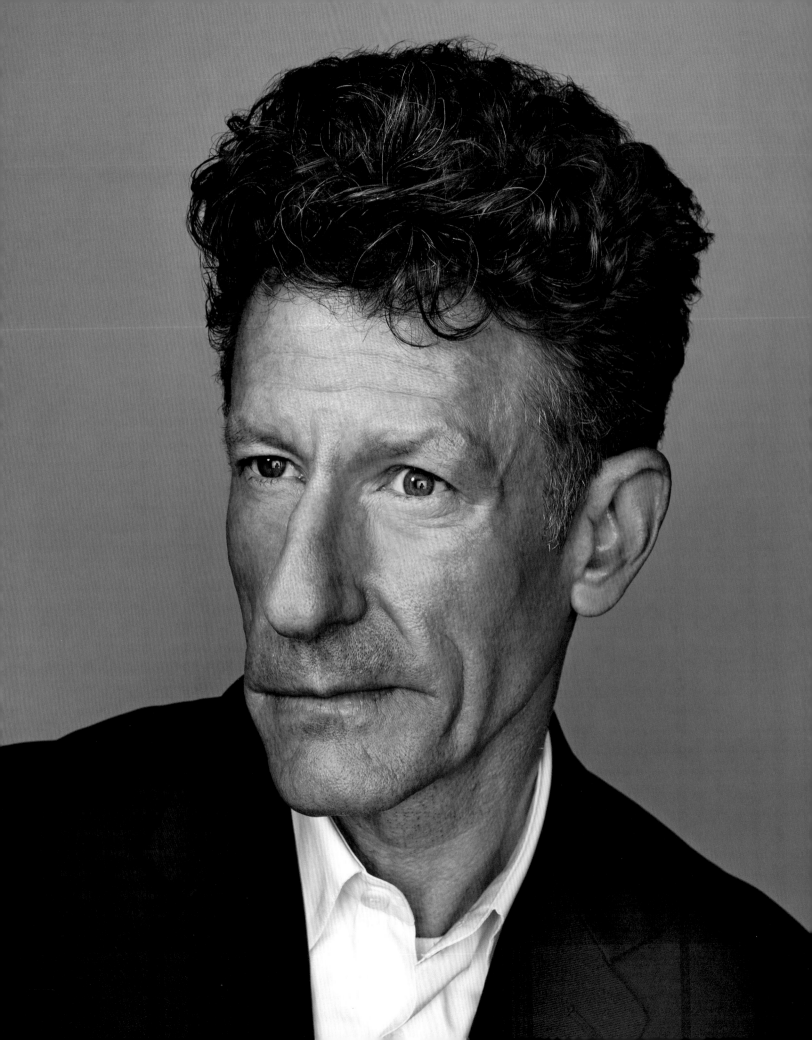

LYLE LOVETT

MUSICIAN, HOUSTON ◆ *Interviewed by Cal Fussman*

>**A MAN** doesn't wear a red cowboy hat.

>**I DON'T KNOW WHAT IT IS** about the shower that generates creative thoughts. Maybe it's the hot water. Maybe it's being unencumbered even by the restriction of clothing.

>**SOMETIMES WHEN YOUR PARENTS** come up the hard way, they expect you to come up the hard way, too. But my parents gave me every opportunity. Much to my chagrin, I was the only boy in tap and ballet class when I was four years old.

>**IF YOU FORGET THE WORDS** to your own song, you can always claim artistic license. Forget the words to the national anthem and you're screwed.

>**SUCCESS IS** getting to do what you love to do.

>**IT'S THE INSPIRATION AND EXCITEMENT** that you get from being amazed when you give a vague direction to a guitar player like Dean Parks—"Make it sound a little more purple"—and then hear him play exactly the right thing.

>**THE BETTER** your bandmates, the better you're going to look.

>**I GOT INTO A SIGNIFICANT SCRAPE** with a bull of mine. My leg was broken. Really, it's a miracle I can walk. That bull was just doing what he does naturally. I learned to keep my guard up and allow him to be himself. That's my definition of respect.

>**YOU HAVE TO BE** really good to get away with smashing a guitar.

>**I'VE ALWAYS THOUGHT** that writing isn't really that hard. It's having a good idea that's hard.

>**YOU DON'T HAVE TO HAVE** anything in common with people you've known since you were five. With old friends, you've got your whole life in common.

>**I JOKE THAT I'VE NEVER BEEN BURDENED** by having an actual hit. There's something to that. My records have sold enough to make the record company money to help me keep my job. But I've never had anything so firmly ingrained in the mind of the public that I'm expected to repeat it.

>**ROSEMARY CLOONEY ONCE** came up to me in the lobby of the Four Seasons in San Francisco. This was back in the late eighties. She said, "I like your music." Oh, man, that makes you feel good. It makes you want to try so much harder. It makes you want to never let Rosemary Clooney down. Ever. Makes you want to make sure that she's right.

>**WHEN I WAS A KID,** I watched *The Mike Douglas Show* after school one day. Buck Owens was the guest. Mike was asking Buck about his songwriting. The familiar questions: What comes first—the music or the words? Do you write it down as soon as it comes to you? Buck said: "No. I never write anything down. I figure if it's good enough, I'll remember it." And that has always stuck with me.

>**DO I HEAR MUSIC** in wine? Depends on how much I drink.

>**IF SOMEONE GIVES YOU** a belt buckle, it's like a piece of jewelry. It has the same sort of emotional significance. It would be something you would intend to keep forever.

>**ON MATTERS OF THE HEART,** one's reason can be affected in ways that just can't happen in any other circumstance. The same sort of thought you might be able to apply in one area of your life you just cannot access from any functioning part of your brain. It's completely unavailable to you. Which is sort of what's wonderful about it.

>**I'D LIKE TO HAVE KIDS.** I'm still hopeful.

>**KIDS SHOULD NEVER** feel unsafe. Maybe demonized by one another, and humiliated, all that great high school stuff that you live through. But they should never have to fear for their safety.

>**A RECORD COMPANY** doesn't keep you for vanity or because they like you. They keep you because you make them money. They might take you to lunch if they like you.

>**THE CONCEPT ON TRAINING A HORSE** is pressure and release. Make the wrong thing difficult and the right thing easy. Put pressure on an animal until it does the thing that you want it to do, then take the pressure off. Whatever the animal's doing when you take off pressure is what he learns to do.

>**HERE'S A QUESTION FOR YOU:** Is it possible to be religious without being judgmental about other people's religions?

>**I'VE NEVER BEEN READY** to do a single thing I've ever done in my life. I haven't been prepared enough, haven't studied enough, haven't known enough. You can never be ready. There's just so much to know.

>**EVERYTHING INFORMS US** about everything else, doesn't it?

BIO BORN NOVEMBER 1, 1957, HOUSTON, TEXAS ◆ *Interviewed December 5, 2011*

>Has won four Grammy Awards
>Appeared in several films, including Robert Altman's *The Player*, during which he met his future wife Julia Roberts; they divorced two years later
>Said "You can't blame animals for being themselves" after being trampled by a bull on his ranch

JAMES MEREDITH

MAVERICK, JACKSON, MISSISSIPPI ◆ *Interviewed by Cal Fussman*

>**WHAT ANY HUMAN BEING CAN DO** in life depends upon the foundation laid between birth and age five.

>**THE BIGGEST UNTOLD STORY** in American history is what happened to the Native Americans east of the Mississippi River.

>**MY GREAT-GRANDFATHER WAS** the last ruler of the Choctaw Nation, and from birth I was taught that my role was to restore the power and the glory to my bloodline.

>**MY MOMMA WAS** slick as greased lightning. She knew how to get anybody and everybody to do whatever she wanted 'em to do. I've always bragged about getting my principles from my father, but it was my momma who showed me how.

>**WHEN I WAS GROWING UP,** we saw ourselves as Native Americans. I was really shielded. I knew literally nothing about blacks. The first time I was called "nigger" to my face was the first day I went to Ole Miss.

>**EVERYBODY ELSE WAS** dealing with the black-white war. Tell you the truth, I was still fighting the European-Indian war.

>**MOST PEOPLE DON'T KNOW** that the Europeans made allies with various Indian tribes. During the period between 1750 and 1800, most Choctaw took European names. My great-grandfather, Sam Cobb, became a United States one-star general. He fought in every major war of his time, including the War of 1812, alongside Andrew Jackson.

>**WHEN MY GREAT-GRANDFATHER WAS** finished beatin' the Creeks, he saw his own army turn against him. The government took his land and his power. He died an old landless Indian. There's a sentence in one of my books about my great-grandfather when he died that I have yet to be able to read without crying.

>**THE BIGGEST FACTOR IN MY LIFE IS** that nobody knew what I knew. I'm not saying they didn't know what I knew. I'm saying they didn't know I knew what I knew.

>**I WAS IN ONE OF THE FIRST GROUPS THAT** went to training together with whites, and I was assigned to a B-29 outfit in Kansas. Now, a B-29 outfit in 1952—that was like NASA, understand? On the first day I reported for duty, I was assigned a room on the second floor of the barracks with a white roommate. When I got back from work that evening, every white, not only my roommate, on that second floor had moved off. Of course, military people can't move without the approval of higher authorities. Not only did it not bother me for the whites to leave, I thought I deserved the whole floor.

>**WHAT I DID AT OLE MISS** had nothing to do with going to classes. My objective was to destroy the system of white supremacy.

>**I THOUGHT I COULDN'T DIE.** And I really believed it. I know better now. But I'm glad I didn't know better then.

>**I KNEW THE ONLY WAY TO** beat Mississippi was with the United States military. I had not just the United States Army fighting my war against Mississippi, but President Kennedy sent in the *best* of the United States Army.

>**YOU KNOW HOW** you drive down a street every day for twenty years and twenty years later someone asks you where that street is and you have no clue? That's what it was like at Ole Miss. I never saw one soul the whole time I was there.

>**MY STATUE AT OLE MISS** is a false idol. And it wasn't put there for my benefit. It was put there for Ole Miss and Mississippi.

>**OLE MISS KICKED MY BUTT** and they're still celebrating. Because every black that's gone there since me has been insulted, humiliated, and they can't even tell their story. Everybody has to tell James Meredith's story—which is a lie. The powers that be in Mississippi understand this very clearly. See, I've been telling them for fifty years how insulting it is to me to suggest that I had to be courageous to confront some ignorant white folks. And recently, they told me they really understand, but they're gonna keep doing it. I can't figure a way to make 'em stop. They're gonna keep on doin' it because it makes it impossible for the blacks there now to say anything about what's happened to them. Because the comparison is with the idol.

>**WESTERN CIVILIZATION HAS WORKED LIKE THIS:** They marched in armor and took over. Almost all of the wealth comes from developing land. England never paid a dime for a single acre. But now there's no more land to take. They've tried in space for fifty years and they haven't found no place out there. So we're gonna have to learn to do what the Native Americans knew how to do: live the good life on the land that's there.

>**TO GET PEOPLE TO SEE** beyond themselves is the most difficult thing of all.

BIO BORN JUNE 25, 1933, KOSCIUSKO, MISSISSIPPI ◆ *Interviewed November 9, 2012*

>Served in the U.S. Air Force from 1951 to 1960
>Became first African American admitted to the University of Mississippi in 1962
>Shot repeatedly while leading a civil rights march from Memphis to Jackson, Mississippi; survived and rejoined the march soon after

HELEN MIRREN

ACTOR, LONDON ♦ *Interviewed by Cal Fussman*

>**WHENEVER I SEE THE QUEEN,** I always think, Oh, there I am!

>**I'M A** get-a-dress-at-the-thrift-shop-but-open-a-bottle-of-champagne kind of person.

>**THE FIRST TIME YOU** taste something spectacular, it's never quite the same again.

>**BEING THE DAUGHTER OF A CABBIE,** I really do appreciate a good back route.

>**PATIENCE CAN BE A GOOD THING**—but not necessarily. Sometimes it's not so bad to be impatient. I'm a little bit too polite.

>**THE BEST COMPLIMENT?** Right after winning the Oscar, when everyone was going home, they let these little gold Oscary shapes flutter down from the ceiling. Leonardo DiCaprio came over, bowed down, and kissed my hand. It was the most fabulous moment—such a lovely gesture. He didn't say anything.

>**BEING DIRECTED BY YOUR HUSBAND** is difficult. But it's fabulous to go home and sleep with the director.

>**I DRINK JUST AS MUCH TEA** when I'm in Los Angeles as I do when I'm in London. I take my tea bags with me wherever I go. PG Tips.

>**WE'RE ALL IDIOTS** when we're young. We don't think we are, but we are. So we should be.

>**SHAKESPEARE WAS WRITING** at a time of great censorship. You couldn't say certain things or you'd literally have your head chopped off. But within those parameters he found great freedom.

>**THE WHOLE THING OF CLOTHES** is insane. You can spend a dollar on a jacket in a thrift store. And you can spend a thousand dollars on a jacket in a shop. And if you saw those two jackets walking down the street, you probably wouldn't know which was which.

>**I DON'T THROW** a lot of parties. I find throwing parties a bit intimidating. What makes a good one? Loads and loads of drink, I suppose. But that can be a disaster as well.

>**WHILE YOU'RE DOING IT,** it's utterly, utterly, obsessively absorbing. Nothing is more important to you at that time and you can't believe anyone could be interested in anything else. I used to come out of the theater and wonder: How can the world be going on? The only thing that matters is this play.

>**CHEMISTRY IS AN ABSOLUTE MYSTERY.** People who really don't like each other can have fantastic chemistry on screen. And people who adore each other can have absolutely no chemistry on screen. It's totally weird—lightning in a bottle.

>**THERE'S NO GOOD WAY** to waste your time. Wasting time is just wasting time.

>**TIME ACCELERATES,** doesn't it?

>**THE HARDEST PERIOD IN LIFE** is one's twenties. It's a shame because you're your most gorgeous and you're physically in peak condition. But it's actually when you're most insecure and full of self-doubt. When you don't know what's going to happen, it's frightening.

>**IT WOULD BE WRONG TO THINK** that you're always right and correct and perfect and brilliant. Self-doubt is the thing that drives you to try to improve yourself.

>**THE WORLD OF POLITICS** never spoke to me because it always seemed to be a world of compromise and pragmatism. That didn't fit in with my rather soppy idealism.

>**VERY OFTEN I'VE DONE THE UNEXPECTED** just to shake things up a bit. That's been a good way to work.

>**I AM QUITE SPIRITUAL.** I believed in the fairies when I was a child. I still do sort of believe in the fairies. And the leprechauns. But I don't believe in God.

>**IT'S SUCH A CRAPSHOOT,** and very often the talented people get lost by the wayside and the people with less talent are successful, and you don't know why. It's all such a mysterious random thing, so it's very hard to give people advice.

>**YOU DON'T WANT TO MISLEAD PEOPLE.** They'll say, "Oh, it's my dream. I just have to believe in myself and it'll happen." It's just not true. Some people throw away their lives following a dream and a dream is all it was. On the other hand, you do have to believe in yourself for anything to happen.

>**I'M IN LONDON WATCHING** the wind blow through a tree, and it's a wonderful thing to see.

>**SOME PEOPLE ARE BRILLIANT AT DYING.** It's hard to stop breathing, and inevitably you get an itchy nose or something. The trick of dying on stage is to make sure you do it behind the sofa or in a dark corner.

BIO *BORN HELEN LYDIA MIRONOFF, JULY 26, 1945, LONDON ♦ Interviewed May 25, 2011*

>Won an Academy Award and a Golden Globe in 2006 for her role in *The Queen*
>Married to American director Taylor Hackford (*Devil's Advocate, Ray*) since 1997. They met on the set of his film *White Nights* in 1984, and worked together again on 2010's *Love Ranch*

KEITH OLBERMANN

BROADCASTER, NEW YORK CITY • *Interviewed by Cal Fussman*

>**MY FATHER CAME FROM THE BRONX,** and anything that came out of the river was usually a missing person. So I never had fish other than tuna in a can until 1998.

>**RESPECT? MAKE A JOKE AT MY EXPENSE,** make it sting and really hit home, and make me look at it and go, "That's a great joke." That's respect.

>**ONE OF THE THINGS DAN PATRICK AND I THOUGHT** was a really good way to pass the time on *SportsCenter* was to try to make the other one laugh uncontrollably—to possibly, you know, snort something out of the nose, to guffaw, to be unable to continue. *You have to read the next highlight because I can't talk.*

>**AS MY GRANDMOTHER USED TO SAY**—and this was abbreviated in the family for propriety's sake—"Umbrella." "Umbrella" meant, "You know, I can live with you jamming the umbrella up my ass. Just don't open it."

>**I'VE NEVER FOUGHT THE WORD** *genius* when people have said that about me. But what it is, is instinct and a set of skills that are working so fast you don't know they're working.

>**I HAVE A LEAFY BRAIN,** according to the theory of the leafy brain. I associate things that many people never put together.

>**A BEAT REPORTER** for one of the New York papers is on a train, playing cards with the other beat reporters somewhere on the tracks of America. The door of the train car opens, and the beat writers see Babe Ruth running down the aisle. He's naked. He runs through the car—"Hello, fellas!"—and he goes right past them. Door swings open again. There's a woman with a meat cleaver. *She's* naked. She's running after Ruth. And one of the beat reporters looks up and says to the others, "So, are you leading with the change in the starting rotation?" If that happened now, we'd go into special coverage. "We need you in the office immediately. You're gonna be on for the next forty-eight hours. Bring some coffee."

>**IF SOMETHING IS WRONG WITH THE HORSERADISH,** it ruins everything. Everything could go wrong, right?

>**MY FATHER WAS** the description of a self-made man. His father told him, "You've gotta high school diploma! Whaddaya need college for? I don't have money to send you. You can draw. What about that? Go to work!" So my father went to night school and found a loophole in the law about architecture-degree exams. Which was, basically, if you can pass the test, then you can be an architect. So after ten or twelve years of doing these night classes and being a draftsman, he wrote a letter about the rule and asked to take the test. He passed the test, and he was an architect. Soon he was sending his son to private school and driving a Cadillac. He had a big house in Westchester, and he did all that out of nothing. He taught me to appeal against all rules.

>**IF I SHIVERED EVERY TIME I HEARD A LIE,** I'd be shivering a lot, wouldn't I?

>**TELEVISION EXECUTIVES HAVE NO IDEA** why anything is successful. This is proved every year by every network. They're asked to bet on ten or twenty shows, and they get one or two right. And then they're, "Oh, the inventor of *Saturday Night Live*! He hired Chevy Chase!" Well, he also hired twenty guys who are selling shoes in Oxnard, California, right now.

>**SECURITY IS** overrated.

>**I RAN INTO SOMEBODY** I knew since the seventies who had to sell his house because his daughter had Lyme disease and the insurance had run out. That's an absolute failure of society.

>**YOUR ANGER WILL COOL INTO HARDENED** passionate insight if you wait a day. Most of the things that make me angry, I try to let them sit. The heat that remains will be sufficient. The stuff that evaporates is the stuff that would have simply offended or made it histrionic.

>**DON'T ASSUME THAT ANYBODY ABOVE YOU** actually knows what they're doing. And if you find somebody who does, stick to them like glue. Because the further you go into your career, the more you will discover to your absolute horror that *you* are the adult.

>**WHEN I SEE WHAT PEOPLE** are being credited for having chemistry on TV today . . . *seriously*? You sit down and discuss what you're gonna do beforehand? That's not chemistry! That's rehearsal. Anybody can rehearse.

>**IF YOU'RE LEGITIMATELY TRYING TO DO GOOD** and you don't have fear, that's courage.

>**I HAVEN'T HAD CHILDREN.** I could still do that. It might be difficult on the kids. I don't think Sonny should have to wheel me to his high school graduation. Or bury me in the third grade or something like that. I mean, it's unfair. Then again, is it more unfair than him not existing at all?

>**SLEEP ON IT.** Write it down if you want. But don't send the memo till the morning.

BIO BORN JANUARY 27, 1959, NEW YORK CITY • *Interviewed September 17, 2013*

>Co-hosted ESPN's *SportsCenter* from 1992 to 1997
>Moved to news in 1997, hosting *The Big Show with Keith Olbermann* on MSNBC
>Hosted *Countdown with Keith Olbermann* from 2003 to 2011
>Moved show to Current TV in 2011; fired in 2012
>Currently hosts *Olbermann* on ESPN2

GARY OLDMAN

ACTOR, LOS ANGELES ◆ *Interviewed by Cal Fussman*

>**WHAT OTHER PEOPLE** think of me is none of my business.

>**ACTING IS LIVING TRUTHFULLY** under imaginary circumstances. An acting teacher told me that.

>**YOU CHOOSE YOUR FRIENDS** by their character and your socks by their color.

> **"FUCK 'EM."** Shortest prayer in the world.

>**A LAZY MAN WORKS TWICE AS HARD.** My mother told that to me, and now I say it to my kids. If you're writing an essay, keep it in the lines and in the margins so you don't have to do it over.

>**I WANTED TO PLAY DRACULA** because I wanted to say: "I've crossed oceans of time to find you." It was worth playing the role just to say that line.

>**WE ALL LOOK FOR THAT OTHER HALF,** that partner. I mean, wouldn't it be great to say that line to someone and mean it?

>**THERE'S 99 PERCENT CRAP** across pretty much everything. And then there's that one plateau where I want to be.

>**YOU EVER GO INTO A HOUSE,** see a light switch, and it's slightly crooked? Drives me crazy. *Crazy.*

>**THERE ARE BASS PLAYERS** who know when not to play. I don't know if that can be taught.

>**BERNIE TAUPIN!** My hero growing up! His lyrics are cinematic.

>**YOU CAN MAKE A PERFORMANCE BETTER** in the editing, but you can sure tear passion to tatters with the scissors.

>**WHAT WOULD YOU DO** if you were a painter, and you gave your painting over to someone, and then you saw it in an exhibition and they'd cut seven inches off the top of it? And the corner was painted red. *We thought it would be better red.* But that wouldn't happen.

>**I ENJOY PLAYING CHARACTERS** where the silence is loud.

>**THE PHONE CALL IS OFTEN** the best part of it. Your agent says, "They want you to play Hamlet at the Old Vic." And you go, "Holy shit! Hamlet at the Old Vic! Wow! God! Fantastic!" Then you hang up and it's "Fuck, I'm playing Hamlet."

>**THE LIGHTS GO DOWN.** What do you got?

>**WHEN YOU MEET SOMEONE,** you can get something out of him like when you first look at a painting.

>**I'M ALMOST INCAPABLE OF LYING.** I'd be a terrible spy.

>**NEW YORK IS** London on steroids.

>**DOWNTOWN L.A. LOOKS LIKE** they started to build Chicago and then gave up . . . and let it become a sprawling suburb.

>**I NEVER MOVED HERE.** I came here to make a film. I've lived in America now for nearly twenty years.

>**YOU'RE TIRED?** Have a baby, then come back and tell me how tired tired is.

>**THERE'S NO HANDBOOK** for parenting. So you walk a very fine line as a parent because you are civilizing these raw things. They will tip the coffee over and finger-paint on the table. At some point, you have to say, "We're gonna have to clean that up because you don't paint with coffee on a table."

>**YOU DON'T STEP STRAIGHT UP** to the front of the ATM line. You don't cut in front of people at the ticket desk. You take your turn. You can learn great life lessons from board games.

>**MY KIDS ARE** my greatest achievement.

>**THEY'RE PROUD OF WHAT I'VE DONE,** but wonderfully underwhelmed.

>**I DON'T BRING THE WORK HOME.** That's because I do the work up front. I prepare. Once you find the character and take it around the block a few times, the engine will always be warm. You just need to rev it up. You're not turning the key cold. You can finish a day, leave it at work, go home, and help the kids with their homework.

>**I NEVER THOUGHT I'D SEE** the end of celluloid in my lifetime, but it seems to be one amazing deal away.

>**BY THE WAY, THE HARRY POTTER** series is literature, in spite of what some people might say. The way J. K. Rowling worked that world out is quite something.

>**A FEW YEARS AGO, MY MOTHER ASKED** what I'd like for my birthday. I had enough socks, slippers, and ties. So I said: "I don't know, get me a ukulele." It kind of fell from the sky into my head. And she got it for me. I started playing it and now my kids are into it. So we've gone ukulear in the house.

>**I DON'T PURSUE THINGS.** They come to me. They come through the letter box. People get an idea in their heads. "What about Gary Oldman?"

>**A DIRECTOR EXPECTS** you to come in, open your suitcase, and say, "Okay, here's my stuff, guv'nah."

>**THERE'S ONLY ONE** authentic version of Gary, and I've got to really know who that is.

BIO

BORN MARCH 21, 1958, LONDON ◆ *Interviewed October 5, 2011*

>Son of a welder
>Renowned for playing over-the-top characters like Sid Vicious and Lee Harvey Oswald
>Currently best known for playing Sirius Black in the Harry Potter films

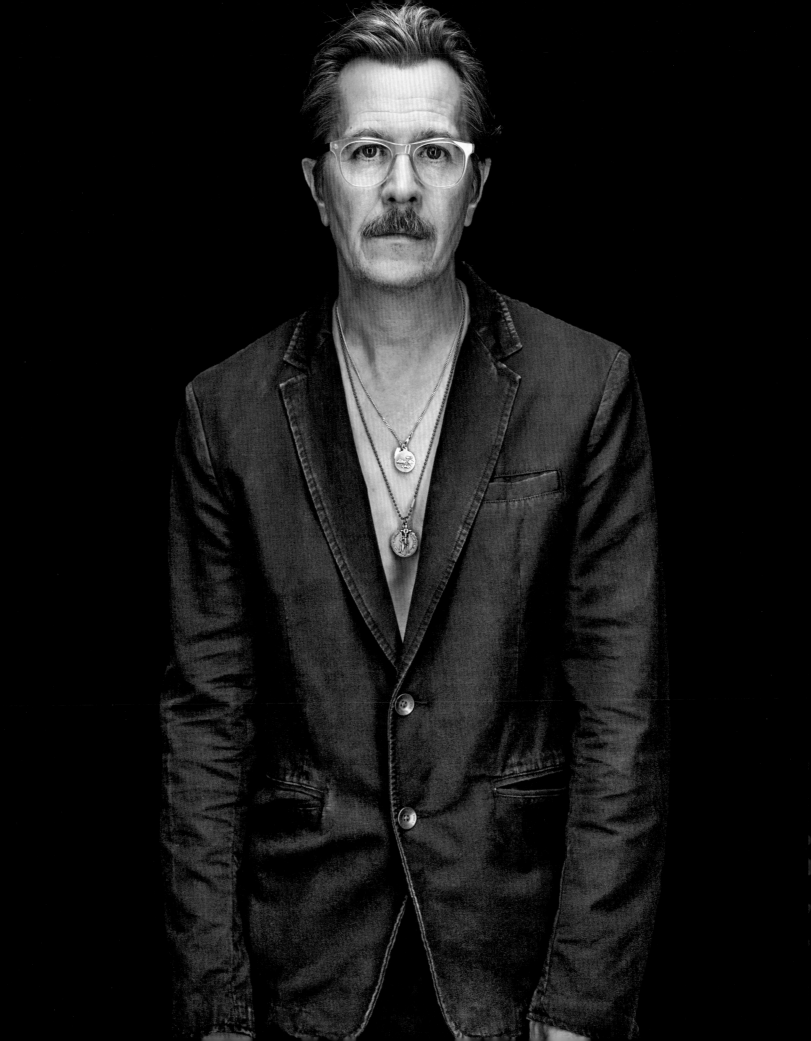

YOKO ONO

ARTIST, NEW YORK CITY • *Interviewed by Tom Junod*

>I'M SORRY, I can't tell you everything I've learned, I have to be careful.

>I DON'T KNOW if I've learned so much from people as from events. Events are the best teacher for us. You try to learn from people, there is always some bend to it.

>YOU CAN CALL IT FREEDOM, you can call it a situation that was not very conducive to having a relationship with your parents. I thought that that was life. It was the only life I knew.

>THE BEGINNING is not all that important at this point.

>JOHN had the best voice. The most interesting voice, let's put it that way.

>OBVIOUSLY, it was a very negative thing for me to lose such a good partner. He was very good. He was a very strong and beautiful and protective force for me. But his words and his music are still here. It will still affect people. And that's the only thing they knew, anyway, when he was alive. So that's the fate of an artist. It's not a bad one. As long as you are what you have created, and what you wanted to share with the world, it's still there.

>I HAVE A BIG JOB in addition to music: to keep his voice going.

>THE MOST FREQUENT ONE that I get is, "Can we change the lyrics to 'Imagine'—No religion, too"? The religious people want it.

>WE ARE ALL gurus now.

>THERE WAS AN INCREDIBLE POWER that was against me. And that power, I hope I was able to use it to do something good. Power is power. It's energy. And if you get big, big energy, you can use that in a good way.

>IT WAS SUCH A WASTE that he had to go when he was forty.

>WHAT IS TEACHING ME is the fact that we have to learn how to turn around negative energy into positive energy. On a very small scale, for instance, people used to call me Dragon Lady. And I didn't answer that one. And one day I said, "Thank you for calling me Dragon Lady, because the dragon is such a powerful animal. And thank you for thinking I'm so powerful." From then on nobody called me Dragon Lady.

>IT'S A WASTE OF TIME to think that if you colored a painting red what might have happened if you painted it black.

>I THINK JOHN was a little more negative than I was.

>IS TRUTH ALWAYS POSITIVE? Of course. Once the truth comes out, you know, it's all right. We're scared that if the truth comes out that it's not all right. It's the other way around.

>I GO TO THE PARK on Sundays. And I see men pushing babies. And it's beautiful. They don't know that John was the first one to do that. The very first one. No man would be caught doing that before John.

>I THINK ONE OF THE REASONS that I'm surviving is the incredible negative power that was trying to erase me. It was not the truth that I broke up the Beatles.

>IT WAS INCONVENIENT, as an artist, when you're creating things, not to have people like it, not because of the work I was doing, but because it was me. It's just an inconvenience.

>YOU CAN BE VERY wild and still be very wise.

>I STILL FEEL that I'm an outsider. About two days ago I was thinking, *It's wrong to think I'm an outsider. I'm just part of the world.*

>YOU CAN'T ALWAYS BE in awe of someone's talent, living with them.

>WE THOUGHT that we were punks.

>I JUST THINK it's wrong not to pursue the possibility of anything.

>I DIDN'T THINK I would be a widow. Nobody thinks they are going to be a widow. And the minute I was a widow, I started to see what a test it is to be a widow in this society.

>PAUL, MUSICALLY, is extremely knowledgeable as well. He's just as quick to write songs. He's just different, that's all.

>I KNEW JACKIE. But I didn't chat with Jackie. Women are very kind of protective of the situation that they're in. So they don't chat. I didn't open up, and she didn't open up, either. We're part of a very strong system. You don't talk for your own survival.

>I KNOW on a very universal rule, hurting people is very bad. If I spoke up, I might hurt some people. Even if those people may be deserving. Their children, their grandchildren—they don't have to feel that there is something wrong with their fathers.

>THERE ARE conspiracy theories. I'm not saying it was definitely just a deranged person.

>THERE IS within me this feeling of guilt because I couldn't stop it.

>BACK THEN, we didn't know anything, really. I look at videos and everyone is smoking. It's sort of annoying now.

BIO *BORN FEBRUARY 18, 1933, TOKYO • Interviewed July 29, 2010*

>Married to John Lennon from 1969 until his murder in 1980
>Mother of musician Sean Lennon
>Remains a dedicated peace activist and active tweeter

>**I'D RATHER** have to put my teeth in a jar at the end of the day than Twitter.

>**RUNNING FROM SOMETHING** and running to something are the same thing.

>**I DON'T GET TIRED** of hearing that somebody liked my work. I'm not for everyone. If I were a beer, I definitely would not be a Budweiser.

>**AVOCADO IS** the perfect food. It's so substantial. So rich. There's something sensual about an avocado. You peel it and then you have to scoop out the rest and kind of lick it. Avocado makes everything better. A burger. A sandwich. It's support. It just backs everything up.

> **"I'M SORRY, BUT . . ."**—no. A qualified apology is not an apology. I can forgive most anything. But I won't forgive anything if it's defended. That's just weakness.

>**IF BEING HONEST** is the goal, I can unzip to a pretty deep level. But what you get today is not necessarily what you'll get tomorrow.

>**BEING NAKED** has a certain element of drama.

>**I'M NOT JEALOUS.** I would expect a man I'm with to look at a beautiful woman. If he doesn't, he's trying to hide something.

>**YOU MEET A WOMAN** who's clumsy and doesn't read, and because of that it won't work. But then you meet a woman who's clumsy and won't read, but she's just right for you. The two can have the same failures, but some ineffable alchemy allows you to forgive the right one anything.

>**MY PARENTS** taught me how to be a parent. But I'll never live up to it.

>**I LIKE TO PRETEND** that I'm a tough guy. It's kind of an admission of defeat if I have to ask for help—or even kindness. But if it doesn't come, at some point I snap and demand it.

> **"I READ YOUR JOURNAL."** I can respect that. Good for you. Everybody would read your journal. But how many people would tell you that they did?

>**YOUR JOURNAL** has probably been read, I've got news for you.

>**I MIGHT HAVE TO GET IN THE HOT TUB.** Can you still talk to me in the hot tub? Would that be weird?

>**I NEVER FEEL** more useful than when I'm making my kids a bowl of soup.

>**MY DAUGHTER** made an amazing jump in the pool the other day. I said, "You're so brave." She said, "No, I was scared." I said, "That's why you're brave. If you weren't scared, you wouldn't be brave at all. You'd just be dumb."

>**I LIKE TO RESTRUCTURE** the rules to make them fit my own needs.

>**I'M NOT GONNA GO** off if there are no M&Ms in my trailer.

>**AT A CERTAIN POINT** you know the last chapter, and you don't want to have to write it.

>**THERE'S ALWAYS** going to be somebody smarter, prettier, nicer. It's better to appreciate it instead of being threatened by it or defending yourself against it.

>**MEDIOCRITY** is underrated.

>**MY KIDS HAVE TAUGHT ME** that I'm not as good a person as I like to think I am, and that I'm not as bad a person as I sometimes think I am.

>**PEOPLE WHO** show up and don't know their lines or come in without an idea just can't be taken seriously.

>**WE HAVE MONET DAY** in the house. We buy a bunch of flowers from the deli, float them in the bathtub, and then paint them. We've also done Dalí Day. We put on mustaches and burn paper clocks. I haven't figured out how to do Van Gogh Day.

>**IT'S NICE TO HAVE** the luxury of not being overburdened with a self-image.

>**THERE'S BLISS** in watching *Antiques Roadshow* and then having some chicken salad. That can be thrilling.

>**IT TAKES MUCH MORE** skill to write something thoughtful than to just be mean.

>**WHY DO ACTORS** end up with other actors? Where else are they gonna meet other people? Somebody who works at Macy's might go out with somebody else who works at Macy's, right?

>**NO REGRETS.** But there have been things that are worth regretting.

>**MY SON ONCE** asked me, "What happens when we die?" I said, "Nobody really knows. Some people think that the spirit"—and he stopped me. "What's a spirit?" "Well, it's a part of you that doesn't change and people think that some part of it lives on." He said, "Here's what I think. I think we go into the ocean, we wash up on a desert island, and Georgia O'Keeffe finds our bones and then she paints them." And I said, "I'm going with your version."

BIO   *BORN AUGUST 2, 1964, FORT JACKSON, SOUTH CAROLINA · Interviewed August 4, 2010*

>Daughter of an army judge
>Won a Tony for her role in *Proof* in 2001, two Golden Globes for her role in the TV adaptation of the play *Angels in America* in 2004, and a Golden Globe for playing Nancy Botwin in the TV show *Weeds* in 2006

PELÉ

LEGEND, SÃO PAULO ◆ *Interviewed by Cal Fussman*

>**LET ME TAKE A MOMENT** to think about that. No . . . no, I have never been anywhere where people didn't know me.

>**THE HEAD TALKS** to the heart and the heart talks to the feet.

>**I WAS BORN IN A CITY** called Três Corações, which means "three hearts," in the state of Minas Gerais. Just before I was born, we received electricity in our house. So my father said, "The electricity came when you were born, so I'm going to name you after Thomas Edison." But they took the i out, and that's how my name became Edson.

>**THERE ARE MANY ATHLETES** who have impressed me over the years. But the one who impressed me the most was my father. That's because I was looking at him through the eyes of a nine year old.

>**RICE AND BEANS.** That's the best food I've ever tasted. And it's good for your health.

>**BRAZILIANS ARE WELCOME** wherever they go in the world. Happiness and the music are the most important things that we have.

>**IF YOU'RE HONEST** and you want to work, America opens its doors.

>**WHEN MY FATHER** hurt the ligaments in his knee, he had to stop playing, and this brought my family many financial problems. I was about ten years old at the time. My mother had to go out and wash clothes to help support us. My mother told me, "Don't play, because your father played and then he got hurt and now he can't provide for the family. Get an education." It was a different time, but she was right. Finally, she said, "You were born to play soccer. You have the talent to play soccer. But you're never going to be a great man unless you go to school and study." That was one of the biggest lessons she ever gave me.

>**COURAGE CAN BRING** huge benefits to those who are prepared.

>**MY FATHER SAID,** "*Don't* think you're a great player. You need to train hard. You need to be prepared. You need to respect your opponent. Only then will you be able to be a great player."

>**A FRIEND** is part of your family.

>**WAS THERE A MOMENT** that I knew I had gone beyond my father? I had the luck to be chosen to play on the Brazilian national team when I was sixteen years old, and when I was seventeen I went to Sweden to play in the World Cup. We won and I was champion of the world. That never happened to my father.

>**THE MOST IMPORTANT MOMENT** in my sporting career came in Africa in 1967. My club, Santos, was doing a tour across many continents, and we were invited to play in Nigeria. The club directors said, "How? Are you crazy! We can't play there. There's a civil war going on there." But the organizers said, "No, no, the people want to see Pelé play. We are going to stop the war to see Pelé play." So they stopped the war for forty-eight hours and they got to see Pelé play.

>**IF I COULD DO IT OVER AGAIN,** I wouldn't change many things. Not for myself.

>**WHEN YOU MARRY** for the second time, it's a renewal.

>**IT'S DIFFICULT** to explain because it was something in the moment and I was feeling very emotional. It was my last game for the Cosmos. Everybody was standing and applauding. *Poxa!* So I said: I thank God for all the love that he's given me. And I took advantage of the moment and asked the American people not to forget this love. I asked them to repeat the word three times. *Love. Love. Love.* It's a coincidence—but I was born in a place called Three Hearts.

>**YOU CAN'T** be scared.

>**MY YOUNGEST CHILDREN ARE TWINS.** One boy and one girl. My son is playing soccer. He's not professional yet, but it's always emotional to see your son playing. I feel nervous that he might get hurt or not play very well. It's hard to watch. Sometimes I don't even go. It's good on one hand to be so loved. But sometimes you want that tranquillity that comes with privacy.

>**WITH SOCCER,** I traveled around the world. I was received in friendship and with affection all over. That is the best prize I ever won.

>**I HOPE** to have your friendship, and that I never disappoint you.

BIO

BORN EDSON ARANTES DO NASCIMENTO, OCTOBER 21, 1940, TRÊS CORAÇÕES, BRAZIL ◆
Interviewed January 31, 2014

>Began his professional career at fifteen
>Won three World Cups
>Holder of lifetime scoring record
>Scored 1,281 goals in 1,363 games, including eight goals in one game in 1964

SEAN PENN

ACTOR, ACTIVIST, CALIFORNIA ◆ *Interviewed by Scott Raab*

>**MOST PEOPLE DON'T EVEN KNOW** they've suffered. I think that's true everywhere.

>**YOU BEAT SOMEBODY ENOUGH,** pretty soon they're gonna either cower and fall or they're gonna be a boxer who says, "Go ahead, hit me again." They're gonna keep moving forward as you're hitting. They keep moving forward against everything. They had businesses set up two days after the earthquake in Haiti. In tent camps, you know?

>**TRAUMA IS A THREAD** through all of it. You know where to apply yourself because it starts to make sense why people do some of the things they do.

>**IN MY TEENS, I FELL IN LOVE** with the movies. And so when I got involved in the movies, I was a genius in terms of how the movies that were made in the generation that inspired me got made—but now the financing wasn't there to do 'em anymore. Trauma. I'm caught in a business that I'm in love with the idea of—the whole process that's possible. Only now they're not making movies—they're representing them.

>**RAISING MONEY** is the very hardest part of both of my jobs.

>**I JUST DID THIS PICTURE** that I enjoyed doing. *Gangster Squad*. But I do think that in general the standard of aspiration is low. Very low. And mostly they're just doing a bunch of monkey-fuck-rat movies, most actors and actresses. And I blame them just as much as I do the business. I know everybody wants to make some money, everybody's got a modeling contract, everybody's selling jewelry and perfume. I'm blinded by it. Bob Dylan said in an interview one time—somebody asked him, *Are you really this reclusive?* He says, *No, I'm not reclusive, man. I'm exclusive.* Exclusivity is like intimacy.

>**FULFILLING** what you start is why you start something.

>**WHEN I WAS GROWING UP** and somebody like Robert De Niro had a movie come out, it was a cultural event. Because he had such a confidence and a single mission that was so intimate. But when people start using themselves as instruments of a kind of consumerist moshpit, they're helping that take over. I mean, you are a soldier for it or you're a soldier against it. That's all there is to it. And we have so little of that intimacy left, it's no wonder that interpersonal relationships have become text relationships. It's a texting orgy. When is somebody gonna sit there, with their mate or their child, and just look them in the eye and say, "I love you?" When is that life?

>**IT'S ABOUT WHO THEY'RE WEARING** on the red carpet. Which always makes me think of Hannibal Lecter. One day I'd like to be able to say, "I'm wearing a guy I killed last night. I've got his skin on."

>**I'M JUST NOT** a big-budget kinda guy, you know?

>**I DON'T READ SCRIPTS ANYMORE,** because at some point you gotta say, "This is my family of scripts. I'll let you know when somebody dies and there's room for another." I'm not looking for projects, because you can look and look and look, but at some point you gotta commit to what you want to do.

>**HUNTER THOMPSON'S SON** was exposed to all that from a very young age, and yet he never got into drugs. Phi Beta Kappa. Very well-rounded. Met a very seemingly conservative woman, had a child—Hunter's grandchild. And they had no problem leaving that child with grandpa Hunter. One time I said to Hunter, "What's the secret? How the fuck do they know to trust you with their kid? How the fuck do you have the affection and faith of a woman that didn't grow up with you as her father? How the hell do you guys have such a seemingly great relationship after all this mayhem?" And he said, "Well, first you gotta keep 'em alive. That's the first three years. And then if you got a lot of love to give 'em, that's nice gravy." And then he told me that the secret of parenting was authenticity. He says, "They might not like your authenticity, but it's authentic to you, and they will find their own authenticity if they are raised in the presence of it." And that's what you're seeking every day: "Who the fuck am I and what am I supposed to be doing here and what do I get out of it?" In other words, "Do I feel alive?"

>**IN SCHOOL I WAS A GENIUS** of the year preceding the year I was in, every year.

>**THERE IS NO SHAME** in my saying that we all want to be loved by someone. As I look back over my life in romance, I don't feel I've ever had that. I have been the only one that was unaware of the fraud in a few of these circumstances blindly. When you get divorced, all the truths that come out, you sit there and you go, *What the fuck was I doing? What was I doing believing that this person was invested in this way?* Which is a fantastically strong humiliation in the best sense. It can make somebody very bitter and very hard and closed off, but I find it does the opposite to me.

BIO *BORN AUGUST 17, 1960, BURBANK, CALIFORNIA ◆ Appeared in the January 2013 issue*

>Won two Oscars, for *Mystic River* in 2004 and *Milk* in 2009
>Flew to Haiti eight days after the 2010 earthquake and cofounded a relief organization
>Also aided recovery efforts for victims of natural disasters in New Orleans and Pakistan

ROBERT REDFORD

ACTOR, DIRECTOR, SUNDANCE, UTAH • *Interviewed by Matthew Belloni*

>**WHEN I WAS A KID,** nobody told me I was good-looking. I wish they had. I would've had a better time.

>**YOU'D HAVE TO BE** inhuman not to be flattered. But it was so obsessive so quick that some part of me didn't trust it.

>**THE WAY YOU** really find out about the performer's seriousness about the cause is how long they stay with it when the spotlight gets turned off. You see a lot of celebrities switch gears. They go from the environment to animal rights to obesity or whatever. That I don't have a lot of respect for.

>**THERE WERE SOME** hairy moments. Some strange dark character was sending me gifts. They kept coming and coming. . . . The guy was obsessed with me and Joan Baez. They had a SWAT team and infrared binoculars, and they threw us out of the house. They caught the guy, and he was insane. They put him away and he died in prison.

>**I HAVE A LOT OF LAND.** I bought it because I had a very strong feeling. I was in my early twenties, and I had grown up in Los Angeles and had seen that city slide off into the sea from the city I knew as a little kid. It lost its identity—suddenly there was cement everywhere and the green was gone and the air was bad—and I wanted out. I went to Utah because I didn't know anybody there.

>**SPEED.** I've always liked speed. I own a car that I shouldn't be talking about because I'm an environmentalist, but the 1955 Porsche Spyder 550 RS is the finest sports car ever made.

>**MAN, IT'S A LOT TOUGHER.** To really be out in nature in a pure way, without being directed, without being there as a result of some marketing plan, just to find yourself pure in nature—I made a film about this, *Jeremiah Johnson*—it is not easy.

>**SOMETIMES** your gut doesn't work.

>**THERE WAS A WOMAN** who was obsessed in the sixties. She'd stalk me and stalk me. Finally they found a gun in her purse and arrested her. She was a dope addict.

>**I WAS IN A SMALL CHARTER PLANE** flying from Santa Fe to Santa Rosa, and the engines went out for nine minutes. You go through that checklist. Then you get down to what it's gonna feel like. *What's it gonna feel like?* I still wonder.

>**I GREW UP** in a pretty cynical environment. All my friends gave each other a horribly bad time. We'd destroy each other with criticisms, but for me it was a sign of friendship. If someone gave me a hard time, I'd say, "Well, I guess he's my friend." I think Paul Newman and I had that relationship.

>**IT DID COME OUT** of the films, and it did come out of the characters we played in the films. The characters—you knew they were friends because they gave each other such a hard time. We'd play tricks on each other. The more sophisticated the joke, the better. And of course, no one would ever acknowledge the joke. If I'd play a joke on Paul, I'd never hear about it.

>**I'LL NEVER FORGET** meeting a kid I really liked in grammar school and going to his house to go swimming. I just couldn't conceive of a house with a swimming pool in the backyard. Did I stay his friend because of the pool or because I really liked him? I don't know.

>**GROWING UP,** I was heavily into sports, and you're given these slogans: "It doesn't matter whether you win or lose, it's how you play the game." I realized that was a lie. You could be the worst-behaving character in the world. If you won, it didn't matter.

>**SCOTS ETHIC:** Don't forgive easily. And I think that's a negative. *Ordinary People* was about that. Scots are pretty tough folks. They come from a tough land and they've got tough minds.

>**LIFE IS** essentially sad. Happiness is sporadic. It comes in moments and that's it. Extract the blood from every moment.

>**NOTHING BEATS** a margarita. It comes close in L.A., but you've got to go to New Mexico or Arizona for the right agave plant.

>**SPEAK OUT** for what you believe and what you feel. Or don't. You have to live with yourself.

>**HUMOR.** Skill. Wit. Sex appeal. That order.

>**SOMETIMES** I'll look at the women on magazines in the market: They all look alike! New this, new that, top this—forget it.

>**THE ONE THAT** came the closest happened at the festival, late eighties or 1990. I was coming into the Egyptian Theatre for opening night. A guy from Tennessee had driven up with the sole intention of killing me. They found the guy next to the box office and he had a gun. He admitted it. He said, "I'm glad you got me. I was gonna kill him."

>**WHATEVER** designs nature, whatever makes it work when you observe it closely, that's good enough for me.

>**THINGS DON'T** work as well anymore. You get angry. I'm pretty blessed to be able to do a lot of things still. But there's an inevitability here.

>**PEOPLE DON'T** remember who the critics were.

BIO BORN AUGUST 18, 1936, SANTA MONICA, CALIFORNIA • *Interviewed January 23, 2010*

>Broke through playing The Sundance Kid in *Butch Cassidy and the Sundance Kid* in 1969
>Won an Oscar for Best Director for *Ordinary People* in 1980
>Founded the Sundance Institute to help develop young filmmakers in 1981 and launched the Sundance Film Festival in 1985

LIONEL RICHIE

MUSICIAN, LOS ANGELES • *Interviewed by Cal Fussman*

>**I WAS THINKING** I might be a priest. To make a long story short, I joined the Commodores, and one girl screamed from the front row, "Sing it, baby!" Afterward, I called up the ministers and said, "I don't think I'm going to be priest material."

>**BUT YOU'VE GOT TO UNDERSTAND.** Look all the way through. After "We Are the World," I got a letter from one of the ministers that said, "Congratulations. Your ministry is doing quite well."

>**WHO'S GOT THE WORDS?** That's the key. If "You Are the Sunshine of My Life" weren't the words, that song just ain't the same.

>**I WROTE REAL-LIFE STUFF.** I didn't write around some fantasy. I wrote stuff like "Easy Like Sunday Morning." What year? Any year. "All Night Long" is all night long.

>**IF WHAT'S HAPPENING** now in America had happened in the sixties, we would have protests like you've never seen before. But in 2011, people can name every player on the football team, but they can't tell you how badly they're being taken advantage of and by whom. They know what Gaga's doing, but they don't know what the government's doing. Everyone's on Facebook and Myspace and Yourspace and Theirspace and Twitter and Tweeter. Great, fantastic! But anybody paying attention?

>**AFTER "WE ARE THE WORLD,"** those three or four jets filled with food looked really huge when they were taking off. And then you get down on the ground and see what malnutrition looks like. When you can't swallow anymore because you're dehydrated. I'm standing there with the food and we can't feed you because you've lost the ability to swallow. You're going to die looking at me with a plate full of food.

>**I WAS BORN AND RAISED** in a community where if somebody can't eat, the whole town goes to feed him. Therefore the community survives. You know when cancer is serious? When it strikes someone in your family. You know when hunger is serious? When it strikes someone in your family. You know when homelessness is serious? When it strikes someone in your family.

>**I DON'T CARE** if I just left the king's palace. I don't care if I'm the poorest guy in the world. I want to come home, sit on my couch, and like my couch. I want to like my refrigerator. Follow me? I want the thrill of waking up in the morning and walking from the bedroom all the way to the kitchen and back to the bedroom. *Ah! I forgot to get dressed.* That's happiness. It's not how many people are calling you "Mr. Richie." Do you like your kids? Yes. More importantly, do they like you?

>**WHEN I WAS A BOY,** about to leave my dad with my friends, my dad would go, "Hey boy, where you goin'? You forgot something." *Oh, Jesus Christ, Dad. I've got to kiss you in front of my guys?* Yeah, you do. Then one day, a guy says to me, "You kiss your dad?" And I say, "Yeah. Yeah, I kiss my dad." And the guy said, "I'm not allowed to kiss my dad. My dad only wants me to shake hands." And that's when I realized how lucky I was.

>**I WAS RAISED BY THE WHOLE VILLAGE.** The Tuskegee Airmen were on the campus. I was raised by the Tuskegee Airmen. The entire mantra to my life was "Failure is not an option." They'd look you straight in the face. "Failure is not an option, young man."

>**GROWING UP IN TUSKEGEE, ALABAMA,** was the bubble. In the bubble, I learned no limitations. My grandmother's a classical pianist. Country music is outside the community. R&B is in the community, and the gospel choir is on the campus. Jazz. It was all just music to me. And once they explained the rules, I said, *Well, I'm not going anywhere near that.* It's the same when your mother says you can play in every room in the house except *that* one. Well, that's where I'm going.

>**A GUY WANTS TO BE ABLE TO** take his kid fishing. A guy wants to be able to play a little softball. He wants his kid to love him. Everybody else wants the same thing, in every different language possible, around the world.

>**SOMEONE SAID,** "Mr. Richie, the show's at eight. We've got a plane waiting." And my dad says, "Son, I want to see you upstairs before you leave." *All right, Dad.* I walk upstairs and he says, "I'm worried about you. Everybody loves you. Every time you go out the door, there's babes." He says, "If you lost it all tomorrow, would you still be the guy you are today?" He says, "You haven't been tested, son. And I'm worried about that." I had no idea what he was talking about. What test? Now, segue. I just lost my dad. I just lost my marriage. And the most important asset I have, which is my voice, the doctors can't guarantee. When you're vocally silent for four weeks—after the surgery, you can't talk to anybody— you have time to think and listen to yourself. *When I open my mouth, who am I going to be?* I could wake up and make rasping noises, which means I'm not a singer anymore. And that's when the strength of that moment with my dad came to me. *I'm going to find out who I am.*

>**I DON'T WRITE RECORDS** for L.A. and New York. I write for between them. That's where it is. Especially when you listen to those country songs. All of a sudden the guy on the radio says, "The number-one record this week is "I Love My Truck." I'm sitting there telling myself, I'm thinking too deep. "Me and my red pickup . . ." God, man. *Just want to drink some beer.* I love it. That's real.

>**I'M NEVER ON TIME,** but always in time.

BIO *BORN JUNE 20, 1949, TUSKEGEE, ALABAMA • Interviewed December 7, 2011*

>Started as a singer and sax player with The Commodores in 1968, ultimately recording "Easy" and "Three Times a Lady"
>Also responsible for: soft-rock hits "Hello," "Dancing on the Ceiling," "That's What Friends Are For," and "All Night Long"
>Has won four Grammy awards

AMY SCHUMER

COMEDIAN, NEW YORK CITY ◆ *Interviewed by Cal Fussman*

>**THE DIFFERENCE BETWEEN SEX AND LOVE** is I've never come from love.

>**I GET LABELED A SEX COMIC.** But if a guy got up on stage and pulled his dick out, everybody would say: "He's a thinker."

>**WHEN YOU DO STANDUP,** you're kind of alone all day. Maybe you go get something to eat in the town you're playing, but you're alone. Then you go on stage and you're weirdly alone, even though there could be thousands of people in the room.

>**I DON'T DO MUCH THINKING IN THE SHOWER.** It seems really inconvenient because of the lack of proximity to a writing device.

>**THE BEST PART OF THE COMEDY CELLAR** is that everybody's just waiting to completely trash each other. I would give every dollar or donate every organ to someone who needed it in the Cellar, but also insult them within an inch of their lives.

>**BOXING IS LIKE STANDUP.** Getting hit in boxing really made me feel stronger as a standup because it's like having your worst fears happen to you. That gives you power because you're no longer scared of it happening anymore. You got hit, and it hurt, but you're okay.

>**THE BEST ADVICE MY MOTHER GAVE ME** was to "Be a lady." But I never really knew what that meant, and obviously didn't take to it.

>**I ONLY MET JOAN RIVERS ONCE.** But when she passed away, it felt like a part of me went away, too.

>**I HEARD SHE WAS JOKING** about her husband's suicide the day it happened. The moments that make life worth living are when things are at their worst and you find a way to laugh.

>**IT'S HARD TO REALLY WRAP YOUR HEAD AROUND** what's going on with Kim Kardashian. She's the closest thing we have to Marilyn Monroe—I'm sure she thinks about that every day. And she has an ass that you need to consider. You can't just glance at it. You need to take some time and think about it, you know? She has cameras on her all the time and yet we still want to see pictures of her.

>**MY EIGHTH-GRADE ENGLISH TEACHER** would tell you that I was a breath of fresh air. My eighth-grade math teacher remembers me as a face on a dartboard.

>**I GOT LABELED CLASS CLOWN.** Teacher's worst nightmare. That was very confusing to my English teacher. But then all the other teachers said: "Oh, no, she *is* a nightmare."

>**BARRY MENDEL,** who produced a lot of Wes Anderson's movies, said to me the other day, "You really aren't someone who's in it for the spoils." And that's totally true.

>**I LIKE MAKING THINGS.** I like working on them. I want people to see them. But I'm not so excited to leave my apartment the day after they do.

>**I'VE HAD SOME FAMOUS PEOPLE SAY,** "Let's hang out." And I'm, like, "I can't. I just want you to like me too much."

>**IT'S HARD TO DATE PEOPLE,** even when you like them, when you just want to be on the fun bus.

>**A CONVERSATION WITH JERRY SEINFELD** changed my thinking on burning material after it's been used. He's like, "What is it with your generation thinking that everyone's seen everything? There's kind of an arrogance to your generation thinking that. It's really not that big of a group who's seen the material. If you perform in a theater, 25 percent of the crowd has seen you before and the rest haven't. So it's better to give them your best jokes." That's definitely affected my thinking—it's just about putting on the best show. Now, I wouldn't repeat a joke I did on Comedy Central. But Jerry changed my thinking about live shows.

>**I HATE ANY SORT OF AWKWARDNESS OR SMALL TALK.** That's why I like comedians so much. If we do small talk, it's like we're doing a bit.

>**I WAS DOING STANDUP ON THE ROAD FOR TEN YEARS,** a gypsy with a lease here and there. The most expensive thing I owned was, like, a bicycle. I just got an apartment in New York. It's the first place I ever owned. I'll never forget. I cooked a meal for myself. A veggie omelet, and made myself a cup of tea. And I almost cried how good it felt.

>**IT'S BEEN A LIFE-ALTERING YEAR.** But I guess every year for everyone is a life-altering year.

BIO BORN JUNE 1, 1981, NEW YORK CITY ◆ Interviewed November 16, 2014

>Made her network debut in 2007 on NBC's *Last Comic Standing*
>*Inside Amy Schumer* was almost a talk show
>Is related to New York senator Chuck Schumer

ARNOLD SCHWARZENEGGER

ACTOR, ATHLETE, FORMER GOVERNOR, LOS ANGELES • *Interviewed by Cal Fussman*

>**YOU CAN'T** learn charisma.

>**THE POWER OF INFLUENCE** is one of the most unique powers that you can have. It's not the power of controlling people. It's developing a certain skill of communicating what you want to accomplish so that people will follow you.

>**I DIDN'T GET IT AT FIRST.** *I'll be back.* What the fuck is *I'll*? *I will be back* sounded much stronger in my mind. So I argued with Jim Cameron. And he said, "Look, Arnold, I don't tell you how to act. Please don't tell me how to write." After I saw it in the movie, I was so thankful to Cameron. That was a good lesson to learn. If someone is a good writer, stick to the script.

>**I WOULD ALWAYS WRITE DOWN** my New Year's resolutions and mark them off the way I mark off sets and reps.

>**ON NEW YEAR'S EVE,** you can just blabber out: I want to lose twenty pounds and I'm gonna read more. But what does that mean? There's too many variables there. If you're really serious about it, then write down when you're gonna lose the twenty pounds by. Is it March 1? Is it June 1? Make a commitment.

>**THE DAY IS TWENTY-FOUR HOURS.** I sleep six hours. That leaves eighteen hours to do something.

>**MY FATHER WAS** a country police officer. All he knew was discipline, performance, and work—not wasting your time. He came from an era where everything was scarce, so everything had to be useful. That's why he was so against bodybuilding. He saw it as narcissistic. His belief was that you build your muscles by chopping wood or shoveling coal, doing something with your body that benefits someone else. But it was from him that I got my work ethic.

>**IN THE EARLY DAYS OF IMMIGRATION,** they just shortened the foreign name. They did whatever they wanted with it. But in Hollywood, there was something else: It had to sound cool. You know, John Wayne. That sounded American, powerful. Charles Bronson. Those are great names. But Arnold Schwarzen . . . ag . . . ager? Ager? Acner? What is this? No one could pronounce it. So early on, they tried to convince me to turn it into Arnold Strong. But eventually the idea became: If someone has a difficult time remembering your name, they will also have a difficult time forgetting it.

>**LET ME SHOW YOU** how far we've come with our fitness crusade: When I came to the United States in the sixties, no one ever thought that one day every hotel would have a gymnasium. Back then, people thought if you did weights you would get muscle-bound and die of a heart attack or become gay or an idiot. People thought weights would always be in dungeons. Now they're in hospitals. Now even golfers use weights.

>**WHEN YOU GET OLDER,** sex may change a bit. When you're sixty-five, it's not exactly the same as when you were twenty-five. But that doesn't mean it's over. It's never over.

>**IT WAS ONE OF MY EARLY GOALS** to be a millionaire. In the beginning, I wanted to have a gold Rolex, a Rolls-Royce, a cheetah—just stupid things that you think of when you're a kid. Then time goes by. The Rolls-Royce thing went out the window, because when you get to the level where you can afford one, all of a sudden you say, "It's a little bit over the top." A cheetah? I think in California they got rid of the law that says you can have wild animals. Having a cheetah is a stupid idea.

>**IN EUROPE,** everyone is in your way. The government is in your way. The law is in your way. I mean, when my friend and I wanted to go start a bricklaying business here, we went down to city hall and got a business license. No one asked: What kind of school did you go to to learn bricklaying? Do you have any certificates that show you graduated from your trade school? Here, it's go out and make it. Just make sure you pay your taxes.

>**I ALWAYS TELL MY ACCOUNTANT,** If you're in doubt about taxes, pay more. No Cayman Island offshore investments. No gimmicks. I love paying my taxes!

>**SAVING MONEY ON TIPS** is nonsense. Give 20 or 25 percent. Wise investments are where the action is.

>**I REMEMBER WHEN** I went into politics, the legislature wanted to create a blueberry commission. Who's gonna say no to a blueberry commission? Well, I said no. I thought they should fix the budget before they do the fucking blueberry commission.

>**WE MUST TEACH** the future leaders that political courage is not political suicide.

>**PEACE WOULD SOLVE** a lot of problems.

BIO BORN JULY 30, 1947, THAL, AUSTRIA • *Interviewed November 8, 2012*

>Won seven Mr. Olympia titles, and three Mr. Universe titles as a bodybuilder
>Catchphrase-spouting star of classic action movies like *Commando, The Terminator, Predator, True Lies,* and *Total Recall*
>Governor of California from 2003 to 2010
>First role post-governorship: *The Expendables 2*

SLASH

MUSICIAN, LOS ANGELES ◆ *Interviewed by Cal Fussman*

>**I NEVER WANT** to draw attention to myself, but that's all I do.

>**THERE ARE PEOPLE WHO HAVE AN IMAGE** of me as being rude and inconsiderate. But I'm completely the opposite, because I was raised not to be. I might have been tripping over myself drunk, but I was always courteous.

>**GUITARS ARE LIKE WOMEN.** You'll never get them totally right.

>**RISK ISN'T A WORD** in my vocabulary. It's my very existence.

>**I'M INTIMIDATED BY SINGING.** I can carry a tune and I can cover a melody, but I just hate expressing myself verbally—especially in the form of a song—to the point that I don't even like to hum to myself.

>**AXL AND I CAME FROM COMPLETELY** different backgrounds. Because of that we made an interesting pair trying to figure each other out.

>**BETWEEN THE BEATLES AND THE STONES,** my dad liked the Stones, so there was definitely an innate gene that I got from him.

>**WHEN I WAS A KID,** I got jobs so I could get cigarettes, beer, and something at the A&P. That's how I see money. It's never been a motivating factor.

>**BEING TOLD NO** was the big thing ever since I can remember. And that was always getting in the way of creativity.

>**I USED TO THINK LES PAUL WAS A GUITAR.** I didn't know he was a real guy. When I got to know him, I found out that if you're really obsessed, he was the guy you'd want to be like. He was always trying to find an answer for what he was looking for in his mind. If things didn't exist, he built them himself. He single-handedly created what I consider "popular music."

>**IT'S A CONSTANT QUEST TO FIND THAT HARMONY,** to connect with it, where everything that you want to come out of it comes out. Those moments are rare, but they're like drugs: Once you get going on it, you're constantly jonesing for it.

>**WHEN I SEE FOOTAGE OF GUNS N' ROSES,** I see that fucking hunger and attitude. You could not fuck with those five guys. It was just raw. It was this lean, hungry thing on its way up. It was as sincere as any rock 'n' roll that I've ever heard, and I'm proud of that.

>**IT'S NOT SOMETHING YOU CAN FIND.** There's a moment you arrive at—there's no words for it. A bunch of people come together at this place where a note hits your heart and your brain tells your finger where to go. It's an otherworldly thing, like when a painter gets the right combination of colors together.

>**IF I COULD HANG OUT** with Jimi Hendrix, it wouldn't be over dinner.

>**MUSICIANS NEVER** actually talk about music.

>**HEROIN IS A GREAT** fucking drug, but it's evil.

>**I HAD MY CHEMICALLY INDUCED OVERDOSES** and alcohol poisoning and all that. I would just keep pushing it and pushing it. I had absolutely no fear of not waking up. But ultimately the clarity seeps through. If I'm going to be here, then I'm going to have to be able to do what it is I'm here to do.

>**MY GRANDMOTHER WAS** really the last person to call me Saul. The people who call me Saul are fans who want to have that personal connection. I'm not sure what the psychology behind that is. But I'm assuming they want to get beyond Slash.

>**IT'S NOT LIKE I'M BRAD PITT,** but I get recognized pretty regularly. The other night I went to see a friend of mine play. When I arrived, there was just too much attention. The hardest thing about being a rock star is *not* being a rock star.

>**THE SPLIT BETWEEN AXL AND I** was a quiet one. But because there was so much attention on the breakup—and are we going to get back together?—it got built up into this monster that led to a kind of animosity that wasn't the focus for me. Neither one of us wants to be down each other's throats for no reason. At this point, I'm trying to put it to rest. So I try to avoid the subject.

>**WHEN IT COMES DOWN TO IT,** I like being with one person that I'm comfortable with and who it means something with. But I have no complaints about some of the experiences I've had.

>**IT'S PAR FOR THE COURSE FOR ME** to find the one girl that is the most exciting, outspoken, and flamboyant—the most crazy. You just have to meet my wife.

>**GUITAR IS THE BEST FORM** of self-expression I know. Everything else, and I'm just sort of tripping around, trying to figure my way through life.

>**NO INTEREST. I DON'T TELL MY KIDS** about those days. One is seven. The other is nine. One is really into his skateboard. I look at him and see myself, and I'm like, "Just do it, man!"

BIO *BORN SAUL HUDSON, JULY 23, 1965, LONDON ◆ Interviewed August 12, 2011*

>Joined Guns N' Roses in L.A. in 1985; quit in 1996 to focus on Slash's Snakepit, and then Velvet Revolver, each with former GN'R members
>Has collaborated with Michael Jackson, Alice Cooper, Rihanna, and others
>Inducted into the Rock and Roll Hall of Fame in 2012

AARON SORKIN

SCREENWRITER, LOS ANGELES ◆ *Interviewed by Cal Fussman*

>**EVERYBODY DOES LISTS** of the hundred greatest movie lines of all time. "You can't handle the truth!" always seems to be in there, which is very nice to see. But for me, the best line will always be: "We're going to need a bigger boat."

>**THE RULES ARE** all in a sixty-four-page pamphlet by Aristotle called *Poetics*. It was written almost three thousand years ago, but I promise you, if something is wrong with what you're writing, you've probably broken one of Aristotle's rules.

>**YOU'RE ALLOWED** one *fuck* in PG-13. The rules are silly. Not all *fucks* are equal and not all *cocksuckers* are equal.

>**I HAD A LOT OF SURVIVAL JOBS.** One was for the Witty Ditty singing-telegram company. I was in the red-and-white stripes with the straw boater hat and kazoo. Balloons. Even when you're sleeping on a friend's couch, you have to pay some kind of rent.

>**I DESPERATELY NEED** the love of complete strangers. That's one reason I overtip. I love when skycaps, waiters, and valets are happy to see me.

>**THE ONLY POLITICAL EXPERIENCE** I've ever had came in sixth grade when I had a crush on Jenny Lavin. Jenny was stuffing envelopes after school at the local McGovern-for-President headquarters. So I thought it'd be a good idea if I volunteered, too. One weekend they put us all in buses and took us to White Plains, the county seat, because the Nixon motorcade was coming through. We went with signs that said MCGOVERN FOR PRESIDENT. I was holding up one of these signs and a 163-year-old woman came up from behind, took the sign out of my hand, whacked me over the head with it, threw it on the ground, and stomped on it. The only political agenda I've ever had is the slim hope that this woman is still alive and I'm driving her out of her mind.

>**I DO NOT DIMINISH** the incredible symbolic importance of a black man getting elected president. But my euphoria was a *smart* guy getting elected president. Maybe for the first time in my lifetime we had elected one of the thousand smartest Americans president.

>**I KIND OF WORSHIP** at the altar of intention and obstacle. Somebody wants something. Something's standing in their way of getting it. They want the money, they want the girl, they want to get to Philadelphia—doesn't matter. And if they can *need* it, that's even better.

>**WHATEVER THE OBSTACLE IS,** you can't overcome it like *that* or the audience is going to say, "Why don't they just take the other car?" or "Why don't you just shoot him?" The obstacle has to be difficult to overcome. And that's the clothesline that you hang everything on—the tactics by which your characters try to achieve their goal. That's the story that you end up telling.

>**OH, I'D LOVE** to get *A Few Good Men* back. I feel like there isn't a scene where, if I could have it back for half an hour, I couldn't give you a better scene.

>**I KEEP THINKING** that I graduated from college a couple of years ago when it was actually 1983.

>**YOU'LL BE ABLE TO SAY** "motherfucker" on network television before you'll be able to take God's name in vain.

>**WHEN YOU'RE A HIT,** you get a little more elbow room and you walk with a bigger stick.

>**EXCEPT WHEN** I didn't have any, money has never been that big of a deal to me.

>**A FRIEND IS** somebody who says the same things to your face that they would say if you're not in the room.

>**BY THE WAY,** you don't have to necessarily always enjoy being with your friends. It's possible to have friends that drive you out of your mind. Don't you have friends that you've had since you were a little kid? And you constantly have to explain to people who're just meeting him: "I've known him since fifth grade. He really is a good guy. Trust me. Really—he's got a heart as big as Montana."

>**I FEEL LIKE** if I'd gotten married once a year, every year since I was twenty-five, there would never have been the same five groomsmen twice. Two new people would always be coming in. My brother is a constant. He would stay.

>**THERE ARE THESE SIGNPOSTS** along the way of getting older. The first is when the Playmate of the Month is younger than you are. Suddenly you're starting to feel dirty because you're twenty-three and she's nineteen and you really shouldn't be looking at that picture.

>**THE NEXT THING** that happens is professional athletes are younger than you are.

>**THEN COACHES** and managers are younger than you are.

>**AND FINALLY,** the last one that happens: I'm the same age as the president of the United States.

>**WHEN I'M DONE** with an episode of television, I feel euphoric for about five minutes and then I'm Sisyphus.

>**ALL BEING FINISHED** means is that you haven't started yet.

BIO   BORN JUNE 6, 1961, SCARSDALE, NEW YORK ◆ *Interviewed September 8, 2010*

>Broke through with his screenplay for *A Few Good Men* in 1992
>Created *Sports Night, The West Wing, Studio 60 on the Sunset Strip,* and *The Newsroom*
>Also wrote: *Moneyball, The Social Network, Malice,* and *The American President*

HARRY DEAN STANTON

ACTOR, LOS ANGELES ◆ *Interviewed by Cal Fussman*

>**THAT DOORMAT?** That doormat? It was a gift. Got that years and years ago. "Welcome UFOs and crews."

>**CHURCHES.** Catholics. Jews. Christians. Protestants. Mormons. Muslims. Scientologists. They're all macrocosms of the ego. When man began to think he was a separate person with a separate soul, it created a violent situation.

>**EVERYONE WANTS** an answer. I think it was Gertrude Stein who wrote, "There is no answer, there never was an answer, there'll never be an answer. That's the answer." It's a hard sell, but that's the ultimate truth.

>**FOR** *Ride in the Whirlwind*, Jack came to me and said, "Harry I've got this part for you. His name is Blind Dick Reilly and he's the head of the gang. He's got a patch over one eye and a derby hat." Then he says, "But I don't want you to do anything. Let the wardrobe play the character." Which meant, just play yourself. That became my whole approach.

>**AWARENESS** is its own action.

>**WE HAD** a scene in *One from the Heart*. Francis Ford Coppola comes up to me and he says, "Harry Dean, why don't you direct this scene?" Can you imagine that?

>**TEN SECONDS** from now you don't know what you're gonna say or think. So who's in charge?

>**I MAKE** my living asking questions, too. Acting, you ask questions.

>**THERE'S NO ANSWER** to what made Paul Newman a great actor.

>**A FRIEND** is somebody who doesn't lie. My friend Logan, great guy, said to me once, "Lie to me once, it's strike one. Lie to me twice, it's strike three."

>**JACK NICHOLSON** could be president, easy.

>**MARILYN MONROE** was used and tossed away. I told Madonna, "You're not like that. Don't be."

>**I DON'T KNOW** why I've never married. Again, I had nothing to do with it. I just evolved, you know.

>**NO, I'M NOT** curious about anything. I'm just letting it all happen.

>**THERE'S NO ANSWER** to the state of Kentucky. Again, you're looking for an answer and there is none.

>**REALLY?** Louie Armstrong said there are no bad songs? I take issue with that.

>**I ONLY EAT** so I can smoke and stay alive.

>**THE TEN COMMANDMENTS.** What is that? That's what they do in the army. Give you orders. "Thou shalt not kill?" And we immediately set on killing each other—in spades.

>**I WAS RIGHT THERE IN THE HALLWAY.** They put a gun to my eye on the side of my head. Three of them came to the door. One of them was out in the driveway in a car they had stolen from a pizza guy. Robbed the whole house. The scariest part, when he had the gun on the side of my head, I remember thinking, "What's it gonna feel like when my head explodes?" It's beyond fear because you're totally in the moment. You're just dealing with what's happening. I said, "I haven't seen any of your faces." And I said something in Spanish—they were Latinos. It turned out to be my housekeeper's son. Nightmare. It's the same as any traumatic situation. You don't forget it.

>**MOST PEOPLE** as they get older don't talk about it. But the sex drive lessens. You're not driven by it.

>**I'D LOVE** to meet Gandhi. And Christ. I'm sure he'd be interesting. And a lot different than a lot of people would think.

>**THE VOID,** the concept of nothingness, is terrifying to most people on the planet. And I get anxiety attacks myself. I know the fear of that void. You have to learn to die before you die. You give up, surrender to the void, to nothingness.

>**OH, YEAH,** Marlon and I talked about this stuff all the time. On the phone once, he said, "What do you think of me?" And I said, "I think you're nothing." And he goes, *"Bahahaha!"*

>**IS THERE** an interesting way to go? Who gives a fuck? You're already gone.

>**THE ONLY FEAR** I have is how long consciousness is gonna hang on after my body goes. I just hope there's nothing. Like there was before I was born.

>**ANYBODY ELSE** you've interviewed bring these things up?

>**HANG ON,** I gotta take this call. "Hey, brother. That's great, man. Yeah, I'm being interviewed by this *Esquire* guy. We're talking about nothing. I've got him well-steeped in nothing right now. He's stopped asking questions."

BIO *BORN JULY 14, 1926, IN WEST IRVINE, KENTUCKY* ◆ *Interviewed November 7, 2008*

>Films include *Alien, Repo Man, Pretty in Pink, Red Dawn,* Cool Hand Luke, *Wild at Heart,* and *Escape from New York.* Also starred in HBO's *Big Love*
>Was best man at the wedding of Jack Nicholson and Sandra Knight in 1962
>Released his first album, *Partly Fiction,* in 2014

STING

MUSICIAN, LONDON • *Interviewed by Cal Fussman*

>**IT'S MY JOB** to sing a song I wrote thirty years ago as if I'd written it in the afternoon.

>**I FIND NEW YORK** a very easy place to be famous because there's a lot of self-esteem, probably more than in any other city. Whether they're taxi drivers or cops or firemen or driving a refuse truck, the people all have their own TV series and they are the star of it. "Oh, Sting is on my show this week!"

>**GRATITUDE IS** the fundamental emotion that one should feel in a state of grace.

>**I TEND TO WRITE** the music first. If it's good music, it has a story.

>**YOU DON'T HAVE TO BE** the greatest singer in the world. What you need to be is unique. Whenever you open your mouth, people should know: "Oh, that's Van Morrison." Or "That's Bob Dylan." Or "That's Bono." You want to get to that point where you have a unique vocal fingerprint. Then it's about refining that sound and making it more and more you.

>**YOUR PARENTS NAME YOU,** but they haven't a clue who you are. Your friends nickname you because they know exactly who you are.

>**YOU CAN BE BORN ELVIS PRESLEY.** But Reg Dwight is not going to make it unless he has this ritual where he becomes Elton John.

>**I HAD A PRETTY MISERABLE CHILDHOOD,** but would I want to change it? No. Childhood made me who I am, and I'm quite happy with who I am. Without my childhood, something else would've happened.

>**THE TRUTH IS** mutable and plural.

>**I USED TO GO TO CONFESSION.** You're asked to ask for forgiveness at the age of seven. But people don't commit sins at that age. So they give you this whole list of sins so you can walk in and say, "Oh, I've got this confession." This allows you to make some shit up, which is a lie in itself.

>**ASSUME YOU'RE GOING TO** make different mistakes than the ones your parents made with you, because you will.

>**TRUDIE AND I HAVE BEEN TOGETHER** thirty years and married eighteen. You can multiply that by seven because show business is like dog years.

>**THERE'S NO SECRET** to a successful marriage. I love my wife. More important than that, I really like her.

>**THE WHOLE ASPECT** of fucking for seven hours is really not what tantric sex is about. But, yes, you can.

>**I'M PRETTY CONFESSIONAL** in my creative life. I'm pretty candid and open about my preoccupations. I'm not going to reveal *everything*— that's pornography.

>**WHAT'S IT LIKE** to sing with Tony Bennett? Just being in the same room with a master rubs off on you. Something happens, you know? You've got to get the ball over the net. So you raise your game.

>**SOMETIMES** mediocre poetry becomes incredible song material.

>**PEOPLE SEND ME SONG LYRICS** all the time. It's difficult. I'm not sure what they want me to do with them. Looking at lyrics without the music is like looking at a one-legged man.

>**YES, YES,** *cough* and *Nabokov* is a silly rhyme. I got such grief for that. But I did it deliberately. It was hilarious to me to put Nabokov in a song.

>**I THOUGHT** when my kids got to twenty-one, that would be it, you know? They'd be out the door. We'd never have to worry about them again. But I have a thirty-two-year-old, and I still worry about him like he's a little boy.

>**IT'S STRESS** that kills you in the end.

>**I FELT SORRY FOR MICHAEL JACKSON** for a long time. Of course, he's sold nine million records since he died. I told the record company, "Forget it, I'm not ready."

>**ALL THESE KIDS** who say they want to be famous, they don't know what they're talking about. You can become famous by showing your dick in Macy's window.

>**AS A CELEBRITY,** you're told how people feel about you, whether they are informed, intelligent, or not. It's something quite rare. Most people go through life without anybody telling them what they think.

>**I'VE GOT THE SAME RANK** as James Bond. Commander of the British Empire. It used to span the whole world, from Britain to India and including America. But now it's the size of a postage stamp. Frankly, there is not much to command. At the same time, I'm kind of sentimental about my country.

>**A FRIEND IS** someone who will tell you when you're bullshitting, when you've overstepped a mark, or when you're being an idiot.

>**I WAS TWENTY-SEVEN** before I had any success. That probably saved my life. I'd had a job with a pension. I'd paid a mortgage. I'd had a kid. All those things gave me an appreciation for reality, and I think that allowed me to still have a career now at fifty-eight.

BIO *BORN GORDON MATTHEW THOMAS SUMNER, OCTOBER 2, 1951, WALLSEND, ENGLAND* • *Interviewed July 21, 2009*

>Has won 16 Grammys between his work with The Police and his solo releases
>Long involved with Amnesty International
>Also plays the lute

DONALD SUTHERLAND

ACTOR, LOS ANGELES ◆ *Interviewed by Cal Fussman*

>**THE UNITED STATES** would have been a lot better off if Benjamin Franklin had had his way and the national bird had become the wild turkey. It's just a different kind of emblem than the eagle.

>**GETTING OLD** is like having a new profession, except it's not a profession of your own choosing.

>**I DON'T THINK** I've ever had a sexual involvement without love. I've never had a one-night stand. Though I was fascinated by Richard Burton saying that living with Elizabeth Taylor was like having a one-night stand every night.

>**MENDACIOUS** people, you've got to see their eyes.

>**ANYONE** who's in a coma, talk to them. Because they can hear you.

>**THE FIRST WORD** I said was *neck*. My mother turned around and said, "What did he say?" My sister said, "He said, 'Neck.' " My neck was killing me. That was a sign of polio. One leg's a little shorter, but I survived.

>**I DON'T GET IMPRESSED.** I admire. I love. But I do not get impressed. It's a fault.

>**MY ASS** was in *Animal House*. John Landis said he filmed it only for the rushes. He promised my wife that he wouldn't put it in the film. But he did put it in the film—and my wife never spoke to him again.

>**IF YOU GO BACK** and look at what Obama's done—it's not as much as he wanted. But shit . . . it's really something. It's more than anybody else has done for fifty years.

>**DURING THE SIXTIES,** my wife at the time was arrested for buying hand grenades, which was one reason I would be audited.

>**AMERICA HAS HAD** an awful lot of wars since 1945. Since then, there's been only a matter of months when America hasn't been engaged in some kind of conflict or another.

>**WHEN A SOLDIER** walks through an airport and I'm sitting in a seat, I don't give a shit that I'm seventy-six. I stand up for that brother and give him my seat.

>**HAVING A NEAR-DEATH** experience prevents you from going into a deep sleep ever again.

>**TIGER HAD AN EASY LIFE** and a very hard life. A child prodigy—going through all that crap to please his father. Suffering through all the dilemmas, the contradictions. He made himself an angel, only he wasn't an angel. Then came the humiliation of that angelic persona being shattered in front of him, shattered by a woman with a 3-iron, and suddenly he's cast out in the desert. And he can't play golf. It's not because he can't play golf. It's because he's no longer the person who *can* play golf.

>**I HAVEN'T FOUND** anything hard about being an actor except rejection, and I don't even find that so hard.

>**YOU KNOW WHISTLER?** The American painter? A great, great, great, great wit. Truly wonderful. A genius. He said something very funny around Oscar Wilde. And Wilde said, "God, I wish I'd said that." And Whistler said, "You will, Oscar."

>**IT'S LUDICROUS,** with the way our life span works, that people retire before seventy or seventy-five.

>**MY CHILDREN** are beautiful, beautiful, beautiful people. They've taught me humility, pride, and fear.

>**THERE WAS THIS** politician in Canada, his name was Tommy Douglas. While he was campaigning, someone yelled at him, "Tell us all you know, Tommy. It won't take very long." And Tommy yelled back, "I'll tell you what we both know, it won't take any longer."

>**IT'S INTERESTING** how many good writers have really good women surrounding them.

>**JOYCE WAS** blind and near death when he was being interviewed in Switzerland. The interviewer said of his wife, Nora, "She's been your secretary, your housekeeper, your editor, your muse, your guide, and now she's your eyes. What do you have to say about that extraordinary intimacy?" And Joyce said, "I would know my wife's fart in a room full of farts."

>**TALK ABOUT** the power of story. I remember going up to the theater in New York at eleven o'clock in the morning on the first day *M*A*S*H* opened. These were the days before advertising, and the only word of mouth was from one screening in San Francisco two months earlier. We went to the theater early to see if it was going to sell any tickets. The line was twice around the block.

>**I DON'T THINK** as forward as next year. Goodness, you're a very brave man.

>**THE SPIRIT** of mankind is not going to help me through my death. My death is a lonely little journey that I'll take myself.

>**YOU KNOW** Dalton Trumbo? He wrote *Johnny Got His Gun*. He was one of the blacklisted writers. Spent time in prison. Lost everything. Got everything back. Wonderful fellow. The last thing he said to me was "Don't forget to be happy."

BIO

BORN JULY 17, 1935, SAINT JOHN, CANADA · Interviewed September 28, 2010

>A legendary character actor, he has amassed over 175 film and TV credits in his half century in the business
>Noteworthy roles: *Animal House, Space Cowboys, The Italian Job,* and *The Hunger Games* films
>Father of Kiefer Sutherland

CHRISTOPHER WALKEN

ACTOR, WILTON, CONNECTICUT ◆ *Interviewed by Scott Raab*

>**MORNING IS** the best time to see movies.

>**I REMEMBER ONCE,** years ago, I was walking out a door—I'd been having a conversation and I was walking out the door, and this guy said to me, "Chris," and I stopped and I turned, and he said, "Be careful." And I never forgot that. And it comes back to me often: Be careful. That was good advice.

>**THAT'S SUPPOSED TO BE** a fact, that the question mark is originally from an Egyptian hieroglyph that signified a cat walking away. You know, it's the tail. And that symbol meant—well, whatever it is when they're ignoring you.

>**WHEN I WAS A KID,** there was someone in my family, an adult, and whenever I saw them, they would say, "You got a lotta nerve." From the time I was a little kid, it was always like, "Heh, heh, heh—you got a lotta nerve." I always thought, What does that mean? But then when I got older, I thought that it was an instruction. If you tell a kid something, it sticks. I think I do have a lot of nerve. But, I mean, I think I maybe got it from that person who said it to me.

>**MY FATHER WAS A LESSON.** He had his own bakery, and it was closed one day a week, but he would go anyway. He did it because he really loved his bakery. It wasn't a job.

>**MOST OF THE JOBS** I get are basically very unwholesome people. There's always something wrong with the guy, and sometimes something deeply wrong. I'm tired of that. I tell my agent I want a Fred MacMurray part. I want a part where I have a wife and kids and a dog and a house, and my kids say to me, "What do you think I should do, Dad?" and I say, "Be careful."

>**I ALWAYS FIGURED** that if I'm gonna be playing these people, that there should be this relationship to the audience that is very clear. "That's Chris, and look at Chris having a good time, wanting to take over the world and sink California and shoot everybody in the room"—just so long as they understand that that's Chris on the set having fun. And that Chris wouldn't really do anything like that.

>**I LOVE SPAGHETTI.** And I like to cook spaghetti. And I used to eat it every day. I weighed thirty pounds more than I do now. You can't— you can't do that. Ice cream—I love to watch television and eat ice cream. But that's like a ten-year-old. I can't do that anymore.

>**WHEN YOU'RE ONSTAGE** and you know you're bombing, that's very, very scary. Because you know you gotta keep going—you're bombing, but you can't stop. And you know that half an hour from now, you're still gonna be bombing. It takes a thick skin.

>**I HAD AN AGENT** when I first got into the movies who said to me, "You're gonna be in Los Angeles now once in a while. If somebody invites you to a party, don't go. Stay in your room, go to the movies." And I have a feeling I know sort of what he meant: Don't show your face around too much. Let 'em be a little glad to see you.

>**IT ALL HAPPENED** when I did *The Deer Hunter. Suddenly*—I'd already been in show business for thirty years, and nothing much had happened. I mean, I really was laboring in obscurity, and then suddenly this movie. It was kind of infectious, and I really did become rather social. Gregarious. And that lasted, I don't know, ten years.

>**MOVIE SCRIPTS** are usually pretty loose—things usually change a lot. But not with Quentin. His scripts are absolutely huge. All dialogue. It's all written down. You just learn the lines. It's more like a play.

>**SOMETIMES I LOOK** at this watch and I think, There's some guy that puts these little screws in there? There is something about it. I'm not into cars, either, but there is something about a really magnificent car.

>**ME AND DENNIS HOPPER,** when we were doing that scene in *True Romance*, it was hilarious. It really was—including shooting him. All that laughing was real. He was killing me. And all the guys around us—that was a very cracking-up day.

>**I LIKE TO LISTEN** to radio interviews. I got a list of things that if I wasn't so lazy, I would do something about, but the idea of having a radio show—two people talking on the radio is fascinating. I'll bet you there's some college around here—they all have radio stations. I get now that I don't like to go anywhere, so if there was some place down the road—twenty minutes' drive.

>**I DON'T LIKE ZOOS.** Awful.

>**THEY SAY THAT** the human smile is in fact one of those primordial things—that in fact it's a showing of teeth, that it's a warning. That when we smile, in a primeval way it has to do with fear.

>**THERE'S SOMETHING** dangerous about what's funny. Jarring and disconcerting. There is a connection between funny and scary.

BIO BORN MARCH 31, 1943, NEW YORK CITY ◆ *Appeared in the June 2009 issue*

>Played Annie Hall's potentially psychotic brother in Woody Allen's 1977 film of the same name
>Won an Oscar for his role in *The Deer Hunter* in 1978
>Was nearly cast to play Han Solo in *Star Wars*
>Responsible for cinema's most memorable watch-related monologue, in 1994's *Pulp Fiction*

SIGOURNEY WEAVER

ACTOR, NEW YORK CITY • *Interview by Cal Fussman*

>**I CHANGED MY NAME** when I was about twelve because I didn't like being called Sue or Susie. I felt I needed a longer name because I was so tall. So what happened? Now everyone calls me Sig or Siggy.

>**MY FATHER** always used to carry his bathing suit in his briefcase. If there was nothing else in it, there was a bathing suit.

>**THAT WHOLE GENERATION** that's gone now, that lived through the two world wars, is a great example to all of us. They knew how to live. If something bad happened, they didn't sit at home, eat Häagen-Dazs, and watch a movie. They got dressed up, went out, caroused, and danced their feet off.

>**I WAS AWFULLY GOOD** as the Cheshire Cat in *Alice in Wonderland*. I think that was in third grade. I realize now that I played it as a screaming homosexual, but I certainly didn't know it at the time.

>**HAVE I EVER** doubted myself? *Have I ever not?*

>**I FEEL SELF-DOUBT** whether I'm doing something hard or easy.

>**BEING TALL** has a major impact in general. It takes some courage to be as big as you are—to live up to it and not be intimidated by the graceful tiny people.

>**THAT'S TRUE.** I *did* live in a tree house dressed like an elf. You have to understand: Stanford in the early seventies was a very freewheeling place. Everyone was doing something different. I had friends in geodesic domes and trailers. Maybe we were the only people living in a tree house. But, you know, you get sick of dorm life after a while. I was living in the dorm with a group of girls who were incredibly conservative. I just had to get out. So I jumped out my window and never went back.

>**YOU GET DRESSED** like an elf and you know you're going to have a good day.

>**COMEDY IS** the most important thing in the world except for justice.

>**I HAD SUCH GREAT TEACHERS** in high school who made me feel like I could do anything. Then to go to Yale, where these drama teachers made me feel like shit—if I have any advice for young people, it would be, "Don't listen to teachers who say, 'You're really not good enough.'" Just teach me. Don't tell me if you think I'm good enough or not. I didn't ask you. Teachers who do that should be fired.

>**IT'S NOT UNTIL** you fight for something that you become who you are.

>**ART IS SELF-EXPRESSION,** but it's for all of us. It helps us understand who we are as a species.

>**THE GORILLAS KNOW WHAT'S IMPORTANT.** Family, play, nature, just eating enough, not taking someone else's food. They live so simply. They're in the moment. When people say, "We're not descendants of apes," I think, We should be so lucky to be more like them. They're so far ahead of us on the evolutionary scale.

>**WHEN YOU'RE YOUNG,** there's so much now that you can't take it in. It's pouring over you like a waterfall. When you're older, it's less intense, but you're able to reach out and drink it. I love being older.

>**I REALLY LIKED JIM.** But he was seven years younger than I was, so I was very surprised when he wanted to marry me so much. I had to lecture him: "I am older than you. I will be ahead of you for every huge milestone in life. I'm going to lose my eyesight earlier. I'm going to fall apart earlier. I'm going to be the pioneer in this couple. So don't ever give me any shit about being older than you." When I finished, Jim was quiet. I probably scared him. That would've been the point for him to say, "You know what, I'm not ready for this." But he didn't say that, and we've been married for twenty-five years.

>**EVERY JOB** sort of teaches you how to do it.

>**IF I WASN'T** in *Alien*, I would've been too scared to watch it.

>**JIM CAMERON SAID,** "Science fiction is the exploration of what it is to be human."

>**I VOLUNTEERED** to serve food to the workers at Ground Zero after 9/11. There were dogs trained to find living people. The people who worked with the dogs became worried because the day after day of not finding anyone was beginning to depress the animals. So the people took turns hiding in the rubble so that every now and then a dog could find one of them to be able to carry on.

>**I GO ON THESE PANELS** and hear people crying because the public can watch movies on an iPod. Hey, who's to say that taking your iPod into the forest and watching a little bit of *Lawrence of Arabia* is not a fabulous experience?

>**YOU DON'T KNOW** what it's gonna cost until you become famous.

BIO BORN SUSAN ALEXANDRA WEAVER, OCTOBER 8, 1949, NEW YORK CITY • Interviewed September 22, 2009

>Took "Sigourney" from a minor character in The Great Gatsby
>Broke through playing Ripley in *Alien* in 1979
>Received Oscar nominations for her performances in *Gorillas in the Mist*, *Aliens*, and *Working Girl*
>Reunited with *Aliens* director James Cameron in *Avatar* in 2009

DR. RUTH WESTHEIMER

SEX EXPERT, NEW YORK CITY • *Interviewed by Cal Fussman*

>**IF A MAN HAS A TENDENCY TO FALL ASLEEP** right after he ejaculates, he should take a pin with him into bed. After he ejaculates, he should stick himself—not his penis—but stick another part of his body to make sure he stays awake and caresses her.

>**GOD FORBID,** he snores.

>**SKIERS MAKE** the best lovers because they don't sit in front of a television like couch potatoes. They take a risk and they wiggle their behinds. They also meet new people on the ski lift.

>**A LESSON** taught with humor is a lesson retained.

>**THE BIGGEST CONCERN** among men is still penis size. I tell them the vagina accommodates penises of all sizes. Then I tell them to go home, and, in the privacy of their own room, stand in front of a full-length mirror, bring themselves to full erection, and admire. You will never worry about penis size again because you won't be looking down upon it. You'll be looking at it from straight ahead.

>**THE PRINCIPAL** concern for women is not having an orgasm. But a woman has to take responsibility for her own orgasms.

>**WE HAVE TO BURY THE MYTH** that Freud taught us – that there has to be simultaneous orgasm.

>**IT'S UP TO** the man to not be offended when she tells him what she needs. He shouldn't say, "I know that!" And he shouldn't say, "The woman that I had before you had ten orgasms without her telling me anything!"

>**IT'S NOT A COMPETITION.** No penis can duplicate the vibrations of the vibrator. And no vibrator can replace a penis.

>**THERE WILL NEVER** be a day when there is no such thing as prostitution. Quote me: I would like to see prostitution legalized.

>**THE TIME** has come when women should pay for a gigolo. Why should only rich men have young, beautiful women? Rich women should have young, beautiful men.

>**IN THE JEWISH** tradition of the Bible it says, "Speak to her softly, so that she will want to engage in sexual activity." In today's world, there's a little bit of a danger in that people don't really talk to each other. You see couples walking in the street, each one of them texting someone else. That worries me.

>**IT'S PORNOGRAPHY** for me only when it involves violence or children.

>**I'M NEVER** embarrassed to say, "I don't know."

>**PART OF MY** success is because I'm very old-fashioned.

>**BOREDOM** is the biggest problem. The same position. Same day of the week. It becomes boring when you don't bring any added flowers home.

>**MOST PEOPLE** at one time or another—when they don't have a sexual relationship—masturbate. They should. But I don't want them to masturbate the whole day. Relieve the sexual tension, then go out and find a partner.

>**I GAVE A TALK IN EGYPT.** There were 250 couples of the Muslim faith. The questions I got from them, about who should initiate, about premature ejaculation, about inability to obtain or maintain an erection, about sexual satisfaction of women, were the same questions that I get here.

>**TESTOSTERONE** levels are highest in the morning.

>**DO NOT RETIRE.** Rewire.

>**YES, I WAS** trained as a sniper in the Israeli armed forces. This was after the Holocaust. I was a very good shooter. I once went with my grandson to a county fair where you shoot a water pistol at the clown's mouth. We came home with twelve stuffed animals and a goldfish.

>**I DON'T LIKE** to see teenage men wearing very tight jeans. The sight of an erection belongs in the privacy of the bedroom, living room, or kitchen floor.

>**NEXT** question . . .

BIO *BORN KAROLA RUTH SIEGEL, JUNE 4, 1928, FRANKFORT, GERMANY • Interviewed September 23, 2010*

>Orphaned during the Holocaust
>Moved to Palestine and joined the Irgun, a Zionist paramilitary group, serving as a sniper and scout
>Studied at the Sorbonne before moving to New York to complete her doctorate
>Her groundbreaking TV show, *Sexually Speaking*, debuted in 1982

THOM YORKE

MUSICIAN, OXFORD, ENGLAND • *Interviewed by Cal Fussman*

>**IF YOU'RE GOING TO BE** a vegetarian, you really do have to like lentils. Otherwise you're fucked.

>**ALL WALLS** are great if the roof doesn't fall.

>**MY DAD TAUGHT ME** to always expect someone coming around the bend on the wrong side of the road, right at me. I was always to assume that would be the case. He tried to teach me to be very suspicious of people—not to trust. I think he took it a bit too far when I was a kid. I had to unlearn that one.

>**IT'S MUCH BETTER** to attempt to trust people until they prove you wrong.

>**I ONLY STARTED SINGING** because I couldn't find anybody else to sing. Everybody I asked was a bloody idiot.

>**TWENTY THOUSAND PEOPLE** can all look like one big mush, but actually it's really interesting how you can walk onstage and within ten minutes feel what their vibe is.

>**WHEN WE FIRST** started supporting R.E.M., there were some gigs we played where people were ordering chicken dinners, and that kind of fucked with my head.

>**I WAS IN HOSPITAL A LOT** when I was a kid 'cause I was born with my left eye shut, and they had to take muscle from my ass and graft it to make a muscle that would open the eyelid. So I had four or five operations, starting when I was very young. I must've started complaining by the time I was five. "Look, you've got to do it," my parents said. "If you go, we'll buy you whatever you want, okay? What do you want?" I said, "I want a red tracksuit." And they got me a red tracksuit, tops and bottoms, and I was happy to go back to the hospital even knowing that I was going to go under the general anesthetic, wake up, and throw up everywhere. I loved that red tracksuit. I wore that red tracksuit until it looked so small that it was ridiculous on me.

>**RESPECT IS** if you're having a political argument with someone, just before you get to the point where you call them a fascist, you sort of step back and wonder how on earth they've ended up at this point of complete ignorance and stupidity.

>**WHEN I WAS A STUDENT,** my bank used to cut off my credit card all the time. I could never seem to stop bouncing checks. I was always on the phone with the bank. It was a very satisfying day after I signed a big record deal, when I went to the bank and paid off all my debts. The banker came across the desk to shake my hand and I told him to fuck off.

>**HOW DID HE REACT?** I think he was quite used to it.

>**EVERY TIME** I go to the ATM and it asks how much I want, I say, "Give the most you can give me."

>**I'LL GO TO THE BOOKSHOP IN TOWN,** grab three or four books of poetry, sit in the coffee shop, and read those for a while. It's like loosening up your muscles before a workout.

>**MY GRANDFATHER** would come to our house in the countryside, borrow one of our bikes, and disappear. He'd come back after dark and we had no idea where he'd been. If he ran into anybody, he'd just ask where the good nightclub was. He did that right up into his nineties.

>**I DON'T FEEL** disappointment anymore. But I do feel the pressure of time marching on.

>**I WAS SITTING WITH MY SON** the other day and his friend, who's eleven, and I said, "Okay guys, do the math. Work out how many seconds you've got left." Took 'em a while, but they got there.

>**KIDS TEACH YOU TO LIGHTEN UP,** which for me was very handy because I wasn't very light at the time. They were a blessing for that.

>**I THINK WHAT MAKES PEOPLE ILL** a lot of the time is the belief that your thoughts are concrete and that you're responsible for your thoughts. Whereas actually—the way I see it—your thoughts are what the wind blows through your mind.

>**IT TAKES A LONG TIME** for an audience to relax on Monday nights.

>**BUILD GAPS IN YOUR LIFE.** Pauses. Proper pauses.

>**GETTING EVERYTHING** you want has nothing to do with anything.

>**IF WE WERE GOING OUT** and just playing the hits and shit, then I would feel very differently about things. But we're playing new things, and some of it's very difficult to play, actually. The idea that twenty thousand people come and watch us do some of this music that's pretty bonkers and certainly not on the radio . . . that's a good thing, man. We played in Phoenix, and Ed and I came offstage and looked at each other. *Did you see that?*

>**I CAN'T IMAGINE** twenty years ahead because I'm sort of here right now.

BIO *BORN OCTOBER 7, 1968, WELLINGBOROUGH, ENGLAND • Interviewed December 19, 2012*

>Son of a nuclear physicist
>Broke through as lead singer of Radiohead
>Formed side project Atoms for Peace with Flea from the Red Hot Chili Peppers and REM's Joey Waronker in 2009

WHAT YOU'VE LEARNED

THE SELECTED WISDOM OF ESQUIRE READERS ◆ *Solicited in 2011 and again in 2014*

> **NEVER BUY A CHEAP GARDEN HOSE.**
> — *Jason Pettus, 31, Atlanta*

>**TRUE FRIENDSHIP** is when you'd go to jail for a month so your friend doesn't have to go to jail for a year.
— *Joseph Carpenter, 41, Westport, Conn.*

> Hang at least one abstract painting on the wall. It could persuade the liberation of your spirit.
— *Maurice Yanez, 63, Sierra Vista, Ariz.*

>**WHEN I WAS EIGHTEEN,** I was shifting gears in my Pinto and I shattered the transmission rod. I had the tow truck bring it home, figuring my dad, a self-taught mechanic, would fix it. Instead, he got a used transmission from a scrap yard and dropped it in the driveway. — *David G. Roberts, 46, Winthrop, Mass.*

> When people with money try to cloak their insecurities with money, it actually makes those insecurities come out blazing. You can't tell them, though.
— *Rett Coluccio, 34, Newport Beach, Calif.*

>**YOU CAN'T ALWAYS** hold yourself to the expectations that you hold yourself to.
— *Chance Ryan, 24, Jacksonville Beach, Fla.*

>**MY DAD WAS BORN IN 1885** in Elizabeth, New Jersey. There was no electricity. Before he died at eighty-four, he saw a man walk on the moon. That's quite a life. But it wasn't easy. He and his wife lost twin three-year-old boys in the flu epidemic of 1918. In 1929, he was a partner of a firm on Wall Street that went under. Then, when he was in his late forties, his wife died of respiratory problems. A year or two later, he called up the nurse who'd taken care of his wife before she'd passed. The nurse was twenty years younger, and they ended up getting married. Then they had a stillborn son. After that, I came along. By example, my father taught me to be happy with what you've got and always stay a gentleman. His name was Fred. But my mother used to call him *Sir Frederick*.
— *Malcolm Halsey, 77, Oakhurst, N.J.*

>**IF A CO-WORKER** is brewing Island Coconut blend in the coffeemaker, do not say, "Hey, it smells like a strip club in here."
— *Yale Hollander, 42, St. Louis*

> **NEVER EAT AT A CHAIN RESTAURANT WHILE ON VACATION.**
— *Curry Smith, 26, New Orleans*

>**IT'S BETTER** to leave two hours earlier or two hours later than to lose your life to traffic.
— *Russell Bryan Love, 44, Santa Cruz, Calif.*

>**CHANCES ARE,** if you're using a pay phone, things aren't going well.
— *Rob Johnson, 27, Lexington, Ky.*

>**ONE OF THE SADDEST** things about Americans is that we're too much in a hurry. When is the last time you stopped to look up at the moon?
— *James Blessum, 21, Des Moines*

>**OF ALL THE THINGS I'VE BECOME ATTACHED TO,** the ones I superglued to myself caused the greatest regret.
— *Daniel Rahe, 30, Tacoma*

NEVER, EVER ASK HER IF IT'S THAT TIME OF THE MONTH.
— *Elliott Langston, 25, Providence*

DON'T EVER THROW SOMEONE UNDER THE BUS. NOT LITERALLY, NOT FIGURATIVELY.
— *Jaimie Graham, 31, Houston*

Just because it's in style doesn't mean it looks good on you.
— *Dean Stattmann, 22, New York*

>**I WAS PITCHING IN A LITTLE LEAGUE CHAMPIONSHIP** when our defense collapsed, allowing eight runs in one inning. A season's worth of frustration boiled over. I threw my glove and spit, "You guys suck!" My dad heard and made me call each player to apologize. I regretted the insult, but I wanted to pretend it didn't happen. I'd have rather been grounded for a year than make eleven humiliating calls, but luckily I had a dad who made me. — *Noah Smith, 23, Zafra, Spain*

>**MY DAD TAUGHT ME** to say hi to people. Acknowledging someone's existence is one of those inalienable things that everyone deserves. No one is better than anyone else. — *Andrew Loane, 24, Brooklyn*

Sometimes your neighborhood bar feels more like home than home.
— *Maurice Yanez, 63, Sierra Vista, Ariz.*

>**THERE IS A DIRECT CORRELATION** between the amount of stubble people will forgive and the neatness of your haircut. — *Adrian Quick, 27, Sydney, Australia*

>**IF YOU FLATTER AN OLDER WOMAN,** she'll usually see right through it. But it will always work. — *Brian Gotta, 46, San Diego*

DON'T SOLVE HER PROBLEM. SHE SIMPLY WANTS YOUR EAR ATTENTIVE AND YOUR MOUTH SHUT.
— *Brian Coogan, 36, Amherst, N.H.*

>**I ONCE READ** that you should always overtip waiters, because those extra couple of bucks will mean more to them than they would to you. I don't know if that's true, but it's a nice thought. — *Chris Gayomali, 25, Brooklyn*

CAL FUSSMAN

People often ask me how I do What I've Learned interviews.

The truth is, after hundreds of them, I don't really see them as interviews.

In fact, I'm pretty sure if I had approached the majority of these conversations through a prism of an "interview" the portraits would've leaned more toward shadow and less toward sunlight.

My approach has certainly evolved over the last fifteen years. I can well recall the changes that transpired after the first What I've Learned interview I ever did. It was with the famed defense attorney F. Lee Bailey.

I had prepared my questions on a yellow legal pad and had them in my grasp—much the way you see notes on the desk of Charlie Rose or in the hands of Barbara Walters.

Midway through our talk, Bailey looked at my notes and said: "I never take a note during a trial. I like to throw direct quotes at a witness, 'Did you say this? And I quote . . . ' If he says, 'No,' I'll say, 'Do you realize that you said just that on page so-and-so?' He realizes that I've just quoted him directly without having a piece of paper in front of me. After a while, the witness gets frightened. He says: 'I'm not sure.' So I pull out the paper. At the end of the day, if he's a sneaky witness, I might give him a quote he didn't say, and he'll adopt it: 'Yeah, I think I said that.' I did that once with the chairman of a big bank. He adopted a quote he never said and admitted liability. The case settled the next day."

I've never put anybody on a witness stand, nor have I had a need to trick anyone through questions. Chicanery is not a wise route to take on the search for wisdom—kindness and respect will get you much further. But after my experience with Bailey I never again brought along any notes or questions on paper. I can't explain why, but not relying on notes made me feel more confident.

The more of these I do, the more it seems as if formality has been chipped away, to the point where every new encounter reminds me of when I was a young man traveling around the world. People I met along the way trusted me, took me in, fed me, and passed me on to their friends and family.

I often bring my hosts a gift, as I did as a traveler. In this case, the gift is a book—a book of these interviews.

The book you hold in your hand is the third in a trilogy and I'm glad that it got published because it's getting hard to find copies of the first two, and soon I would've run out of gifts.

Many of the subjects had written books of their own, and I'd bring one of their books along with me, and after our conversation we'd sign copies to each other as a memory of our time together.

Two of the more recent exchanges now make me smile. The first came from Woody Allen, who signed *The Insanity Defense* like this: "Thank you for your book. I'm sure it's more interesting than mine."

The second is what Tony Bennett wrote above a drawing he'd done of Frank Sinatra on the pages of his memoir, *Life is a Gift*: "To Cal, Thank you for the best interview I've ever had."

I'm not sure if either of those inscriptions is accurate. But what I like about them is that Woody opened up to me—even inviting me afterward to a stand-up comedy performance taking place the next night—without knowing my name.

And I'm fairly certain that Tony wrote what he did for a simple reason: because our conversation didn't seem like an interview at all.

SCOTT RAAB

I talked to Christopher Walken at his house in Connecticut. He met me at the door, in his bathrobe. Cool cat. This guy was a Broadway hoofer as a child, and a lion tamer at the age of sixteen—"She was very sweet, really like an old dog"— and much of his movie work, big and small, is unforgettable, and it's a late winter morning draped in gloom, chilly wet, but the old house is warm and he's in the middle of brewing coffee. Nice.

"This is going to be very strong," he says when he puts my cup in front of me at the dining room table.

Good coffee. Walken's maybe the easiest guy I've ever sat down and talked with. He's worried, though, that he lacks sufficient gravitas for a What I've Learned.

"I jotted down a couple of things," he says. "I thought about it. I never think about things like that, but I thought, 'Sure, I've learned some things.' But they're very simple things. And I'm not sure that I learned them."

"We don't have to shoot for the cosmic here," I tell him.

We wind up talking for a couple of hours, and it's great. Hell, much of the cutting-room floor stuff—meeting Fred Astaire and Gene Kelly, hanging out at Warhol's Factory, working with Dennis Hopper and James Gandolfini on *True Romance*—is pure gold. But he keeps on worrying about coming up short on the wisdom scale, even as I'm on my way out the door.

"It's very hard to talk about stuff like that—I mean, just to figure it out in the first place. But if that's what the interview's about—wisdom—be careful, use seatbelts, 55 saves lives. That's my wisdom. Drink your orange juice."

TOM JUNOD

There was always a double-consciousness at work when I interviewed Yoko Ono at her apartment at the Dakota. It was not just an apartment; it was *that* apartment, and so when a butler opened the door, advanced in years and dressed in a white jacket, I wondered if he was *that* butler, who had nursed John through his binges and dry spells and domestic joys. When the butler bid me take off my shoes, I stepped on a silvery white carpet so sumptuous it seemed to exert a kind of suction on the soles of my bare feet . . . but surely it couldn't be *that* carpet, although the white piano that loomed before me when I sat on the couch and drank a cup of tea was very much *that* piano, where John had written "Imagine." And so it went. I had been warned, beforehand, that Yoko likes to flash reporters her cleavage, and sure enough, when she entered the room, she wore a black sweat shirt with the word "Berlin" printed across the front, except that her zipper was pulled down so low the word was split down the middle like the city itself had once been: "BER" and "LIN." She was by this time seventy-seven years old, but it seemed to be *that* cleavage, and indeed she was more genuine than I ever expected her to be. I was enduring some family trials at the time, and she spoke to me of her own experience, though it was clear, after a while, that she had two families, one comprised of Sean and the other of Paul and Ringo, and that she had reconciled with the first and was very wary of the second. Indeed, she asked me not to write about her feelings about the Beatles and about the details of the art on her walls, which was museum quality. What I can't refrain from writing about, however, is something I saw as I was leaving—an Egyptian sarcophagus, in all its funereal splendor. It was a reminder of sorts, not just of death but of *that* death, the one that haunted *that* apartment, because it involved *that* Beatle, who had written that song on *that* white piano, a sarcophagus all its own.

RYAN D'AGOSTINO

Tall man, Elliott Gould.

When he opened the door to his hotel room, he filled the space. He was wearing shorts. He was still tall when he sat down. After my first question, he paused—a long pause, terrifying for me. My question wasn't even really a question, just a dumb opening line about the retrospective of his early films that the local film center was putting on, and what an interesting experience that must be at this point in his life. And he didn't say anything. I thought, *He thinks I'm an idiot*. But after that excruciating minute he looked and said, soft and deliberate, "I don't know what's early or what's late in relation to a life." And he talked for eight-and-a-half minutes straight, about human evolution, the challenge of confidence, Mick Jagger, "accessing and experiencing the intelligence of nature," Donald Sutherland, and the power of a hot bath. The rest of the interview was filled with these long silences before he spoke. But it got a little less terrifying each time, because even if he thought I was an idiot, he was only pausing because, in what could have been the hundred-thousandth interview of his career, he really and truly wanted to share what he had learned in his life. He was just thinking.

After the interview, we rode the subway.

MIKE SAGER

Ethan Hawke arrived early at the Esquire offices a little breathless. It was the morning after the magazine's big 80th anniversary celebration. Waiting across the hall was a roomful of editors and publishers from the 27 different international editions of Esquire. Hawke had graciously consented to be interviewed on stage.

"You've got to excuse me," he said dramatically, his blue eyes lit. "I was woken before dawn by my five year old. She was like, 'Daddy, Daddy. There's been a storm downstairs.'"

"And I'm like, 'What do you mean?'"

"And she says, 'The house is full of smoke and water.'"

"And I say, 'No it's not, baby, go back to sleep.'"

But little Clementine Jane Hawke, the third of his four children, aged two through fifteen, was not to be otherwise convinced.

The family lives in a single-family town house. The bedrooms are upstairs. The kitchen and dining room are on the parlor floor. The living area is in the basement.

"We go downstairs to the kitchen," Hawke said, "and sure enough, it's a disaster. Somehow our icemaker had malfunctioned and water was pouring all night long. The entire floor had fallen into the basement."

Assessing the damage, noting the weight of his schedule—our interview, his ongoing rehearsals for *Macbeth* on Broadway—our fearless actor/homeowner marched back upstairs and did what any man in his situation might do.

He went and woke up his wife.

JOHN H. RICHARDSON

My first thought: what a crappy place for an interview.

I was waiting for Samuel L. Jackson in a giant photography loft in midtown Manhattan with an acre of windows facing the Hudson River and nothing in it except one chair and a sofa, as sterile and unrelaxing a location as possible—a setting for an interrogation.

Then Jackson came in and filled the room. The effect was striking and immediate. He didn't shout or wave his arms or do accents. He didn't try to "connect." He was calm, relaxed, and professional. But as he talked about his remarkable life—occupying his college administration's office in the thick of the civil rights era, serving as an usher in Martin Luther King's funeral, losing himself to crack cocaine and finding his way back to a life of decency and hard work.

There was a solidity to him that was so damn solid it seemed to crackle and expand. That's what you see on screen, something as rare in Hollywood as it is in life: a man big enough to fill the frame and sane enough to enjoy every second.

ROSS MCCAMMON

The overriding memory of my interview with 50 Cent was construction noise. The G-Unit record label offices at 41st Street and 8th Avenue were in the middle of being renovated. His entire staff was wedged into one or two rooms, and the only available space was a room under construction. Construction workers walked in and out. There was sawing, drilling, hammering. Worst possible interview conditions.

"So, tell me about your mother—" [SOUND OF ANGLE GRINDER]

Awful.

I'm sure I'm forgetting some introductory niceties, but I recall that his first words were: "This is going to be an interesting interview." Here's a tip if you're ever interviewed by a journalist: Say that. I. It disarms them. 2. It sets a minimum requirement. And it made the chaos going on around us recede a little. It was a generous thing to say, and it was the first of many kindnesses.

The one kindness I appreciated the most was: every time the drilling, hammering, grinding would start up, he would grab the recording device and hold it up to his mouth as he spoke. It was a subtle, thoughtful, helpful thing. And it suggested that he was a partner as much as a subject.

Correction: The overriding memory of the interview was that 50 Cent was a sweetheart.

MATTHEW BELLONI

Interviewing Robert Redford at the Sundance Film Festival is a little like trying to nail down the Pope on Easter Sunday.

So when his flack promised he could carve out a few hours during the frenzy of the January indie film fest for an interview, I was skeptical. Worse, they wanted to do the sit-down in a filmmaker lounge that would be bustling with nervous directors hoping their movies become the next *sex lies and videotape* or *Beasts of the Southern Wild*.

When Redford arrived, however, he was the consummate pro—being famous for 50 years will sharpen a man's press skills—talking politics, Newman, Watergate, whatever. Then the flack materialized about 45 minutes in to announce that "Bill Gates would like to say hello." *OK*, I thought, *interview over*. And I was right. Gates, in Park City as a backer of the education documentary *Waiting for Superman*, is apparently a huge *Sundance Kid* fan and had never met the man himself. This was going to be awhile, I thought, and I was fine with that. Bill Gates and Robert Redford should know each other, I thought. Some good will no doubt come of this.

So, as they began chatting, I politely excused myself and rescheduled for a few hours in his (quiet) office the next day.

INDEX

PHOTO CREDITS

© Corey Arnold: 42
AUGUST: © Austin Hargrave: 67
© Miriam Berkley: 76
© Darrell Blakely: 101
© Chris Buck: 32, 34, 38
© Francesco Carrozzini: 47
© Chuck Close in association with Jerry Spagnoli, courtesy
Pace Gallery: 70
© Comedy Central: Peter Yang: 120
Corbis: © Denis O'Regan: 130
Corbis Outline: © Eric Johnson: 85; © Gregg Segal: 24; © Ben
Watts: 8
CPi Syndication: © Nigel Parry: 20, 54, 56, 59, 114
Getty Images: © Michael Friberg/Contour by Getty: 78; © GAB
Archive/Redferns: 64; © Ron Galella/WireImage: 90; © Chris
McKay: 48; © Michael Ochs Archive: 96; © Tony Tomsic: 28
Globe Photos: © Jay Thompson: 117
© Marco Grob: 86
© Brantley Gutierrez: 60
© Kurt Iswarienko: 132
© Sam Jones: 72, 122
© Michael Kelley: 26
© Gillian Laub: 62

© Michael Lavine: 23, 88
© Ture Lillegraven: 10, 75, 126
© Alexi Lubomirski/Management+Artists: 95
© Mark Mann: 13
© Robert Maxwell: 107
© Jeff Minton: 52, 118
© Miller Mobley: 104
© Perou: 102
Photofest: 92
© Ramona Rosales: 80
© Emily Shur: 44
© Angela Talley: 50
Trunk Archive: © Bryan Adams: 18; © Jake Chessum: 17, 138;
© Simon Emmett: 36, 112; © Marco Grob: 41; © Peter Hapak: 82;
© NadavKander: 141; © Cliff Watts: 136
© Frank Veronsky: 31
© 2015 The Andy Warhol Foundation for the Visual Arts, Inc./
Artists Rights Society (ARS), New York: 108
© Victoria Will: 125
© Robert Todd Williamson: 110
© Dan Winters: 128
© Peter Yang: 98, 135
© Zach Wolfe: 146

HEARST BOOKS
New York

An Imprint of Sterling Publishing
1166 Avenue of the Americas
New York, NY 10036

ISBN 978-1-61837-165-2

Distributed in Canada by Sterling Publishing
c/o Canadian Manda Group, 664 Annette Street
Toronto, Ontario, Canada M6S 2C8
Distributed in the United Kingdom by GMC Distribution Services
Castle Place, 166 High Street, Lewes, East Sussex, England BN7 1XU
Distributed in Australia by Capricorn Link (Australia) Pty. Ltd.
P.O. Box 704, Windsor, NSW 2756, Australia

For information about custom editions, special sales, and premium and corporate purchases,
please contact Sterling Special Sales at 800-805-5489 or specialsales@sterlingpublishing.com.

Manufactured in China

2 4 6 8 10 9 7 5 3 1

www.sterlingpublishing.com